Me & You

For Joe

Anita Naik is a freelance writer who writes for *New Woman*, *Eve*, *Zest*, *Red*, *Cosmopolitan* and *Glamour*. Specialising in health, relationship and lifestyle issues, Anita was also the advice columnist on *Just 17*, the sex columnist on *More* and is currently an advice columnist on *Closer* magazine.

Anita is also the author of:

The Lazy Girl's Guide to Beauty

The Lazy Girl's Guide to Good Health

The Lazy Girl's Guide to Good Sex

The Lazy Girl's Guide to a Fabulous Body

The Lazy Girl's Party Guide

Babe Bible

The New You

CHANGE YOUR LIFE IN A MONTH

ANITA NAIK

PIATKUS

✿ *Visit the Piatkus website!*

Piatkus publishes a wide range of best-selling fiction and non-fiction, including books on health, mind, body & spirit, sex, self-help, cookery, biography and the paranormal.

If you want to:
- read descriptions of our popular titles
- buy our books over the Internet
- take advantage of our special offers
- enter our monthly competition
- learn more about your favourite Piatkus authors

VISIT OUR WEBSITE AT: **www.piatkus.co.uk**

Copyright © 2005 by Anita Naik
www.anitanaik.co.uk

First published in 2005 by
Piatkus Books Ltd
5 Windmill Street
London W1T 2JA

e-mail: info@piatkus.co.uk

The moral right of the author has been asserted

A catalogue record for this book is available from the British Library

ISBN 0 7499 2631 7

Text design and setting by Vivid Design
Edited by Jan Cutler

This book has been printed on paper manufactured with respect for the environment using wood from managed sustainable resources

Data manipulation by Phoenix Photosetting, Chatham, Kent
Printed and bound in China by Everbest Printing Co Ltd

Contents

To all the people who inspired, helped
and encouraged me to find the new me,
especially Joe R, Judy C, Jenni B, Emma B
and my parents.

Introduction

My story

Are you addicted to self help programmes, change your life books and costly expert gurus who promise to revolutionise your life? If so, you're not alone. Not only have I been there and done that but also statistics show that the majority of people around you have done so, too. According to new figures the self-help industry in the UK alone is now worth around £15 billion a year (add the USA, Australia and the rest of the world to spiral this figure into the beyond), due to the increasing number of us who desperately 'need' the advice of an army of high-level fixers.

The trouble is that finding the new you is expensive. I know, because just 12 years ago I spent copious amounts on 'finding the new and improved me'. At 24 I was the typical example of a doctor who wouldn't take her own medicine – except I was an advice columnist who wouldn't take her own advice. I had a successful career on a magazine, an extensive social life that involved expensive restaurants and travels to exotic far-off places, and what looked like the 'perfect' boyfriend.

Yet, what most people didn't know was that I was depressed by my life. I had large debts, thanks to living beyond my means on credit cards and loans. I was unhappy with the direction my career and body were taking (think downward) and my 'perfect' boyfriend was, let's just say, less than good, never mind less than perfect.

Being a self-aware kind of girl, my solution was to do what any sane woman would do: go and seek expert advice. So off I went to see clairvoyants who told me what I wanted to hear, New Age gurus who told me to chant, and offbeat visionaries who told me all my life lessons were karmic. I tried positive affirmations in front of a mirror for better self-esteem and went through lymph drainage and spiritual healing for a clearer mind and stronger body. I handed over half my monthly wage to go on a weekend self-help course with 20,000 other people where I jumped up and down and screamed 'YES' (to what I can hardly remember).

I also tried every celebrity diet going, crash/miracle diets and even the coffee-and-doughnut-only diet. I also immersed myself in hundreds of self-help books, all along the lines of 'read this feel the love fight the fear and get fixed in seven easy steps while cleaning out your cupboards!' and then bored friends rigid with the latest solution to all my problems (and theirs).

I wish I could say that one day I woke up and found I'd been transformed. Unfortunately, one day I woke up even more depressed than usual and took to my bed for three days. Help came in the revelation that it was time for a reality check, and that the reality burst I needed was a practical plan. So out went the hopeless boyfriend and the idea that salvation could be found in shoes that cost more than my monthly rent, and in came the real experts: people like my beleaguered bank manager, the personal trainers at my local gym, and even friends who had successfully tackled their own demons.

Shock number one was realising that there was pleasure to be had in sorting out my life in a practical rather than esoteric way. By opening my bank statements, cutting up my credit cards and looking at the state of my health and habits I stopped whining, 'What will become of me?' and woke up to what would actually happen to me if I didn't change my ways.

The second shock was that facing my messes wasn't about punishment and self-deprivation, but about being honest and finding workable solutions that I could maintain and follow.

A decade further along the line I have learnt how to get out of debt, build up a healthy financial portfolio and how to double my income and turn my career around. Even better, I know how to get fit in a way that's healthy and lasting, and even how to fall in love for keeps. 'Smug so and so', I hear you cry. Well, not really – a lot of it was hard work (and still is) but I do now know that no matter how many years of living badly, it is possible to kick-start change and find a new way of living. More importantly, although it takes time to reach your goals, all the hard stuff happens in the first month.

Of course, this doesn't mean you can lose 2 stone (13kg/28lb) in a month, create a financial portfolio akin to Donald Trump in four weeks, or even find the partner of your dreams by the time your next payday comes around. It took me four years to build a healthy amount of savings and get out of debt for good, two years to be fit enough to run happily every day, and the process of finding career successes is ongoing, but – and this is a big BUT – it took only four weeks to make the essential adjustments that changed everything in my life.

That's four weeks to decide to leave my job, and ignore the critics who yelled, 'What are you doing?' Four weeks to discover that I had a bigger entrepreneurial spirit than I previously thought. Four weeks to cut up my life-saving (but ultimately life-ruining) credit cards, and four weeks to work out a financial plan that leaves me happily debt-free today. It also took only a month to get over the I-can't-face-this-diet-for-one-more-day state of mind, and one month to get into the habit of doing an hour's exercise every day.

As someone once said, 'All changes begin with an ending' – and that ending is about giving up the old and tired you and deciding in an instant to move onwards and upwards. So, whether you're here because you're close to despair, or are simply looking for the inside track to a new life, you've come to the right place. This is a makeover book with a difference. Each section will help you to identify the habits that are personally holding YOU back, because, let's face it, one person's, 'I'm in debt because I blow money on drink each night' is another person's, 'I'm in debt because I buy 500 pairs of shoes each week.'

For this reason *The New You* also has a one-month day-by-day plan to help you bust bad habits and create new ones. So, if you've lost your way, or feel some doors are now closed to your for ever due to your age, circumstances or mindset, give this book a try and discover the new you. What have you got to lose?

Anita

Body

Introduction

Unhappy with the way your body looks? Sick of feeling fat and out of shape? Tired of hiding in corners at parties and pretending you're fine when you're not? If you're reading this section I'm guessing this is you and you're looking for help on how to change. If so, it's worth knowing that no matter how depressed and discouraged you feel right now, a new body is within your grasp. If you don't believe me, start by looking at all the hundreds of people who lose weight every day. Despite small differences in lifestyle at some point they were where you are right now.

Of course, you may have a hundred reasons why you personally can't do it – maybe you have no time, no willpower, no help and/or no idea how to say no to the fattening and comforting food you love to eat. Or maybe you just feel so despondent that to try to lose weight again feels like a failure in itself. If any of these ring true, it's time to stop and rethink your position. Telling yourself why you can't do something only reinforces that thought in your head and stops you from moving forwards, and, let's face it, we're all creatures of habit and tend to do what feels safe and comfortable, even if those safe and comfortable things keep us in a place that makes us unhappy.

So, this time around, change the record and start telling yourself you can do it. Forget the past, today is the first day of the rest of your life, which means it's time to concentrate on the task in hand. First and foremost you need to inspire yourself. Research shows we are more likely to reach our goals if we have a clear idea of what that goal looks like, tastes like and feels like. Meaning, close your eyes and spend a few minutes imagining the fitter and leaner you of the future. What do you look like? What clothes are you wearing? What opportunities are you grabbing, what experiences are you trying out? And how do you feel?

Hold on to this because this is your motivating goal that will drive you forward to change. Having said that, keep the vision realistic; no amount of fitness will turn you into a supermodel who looks 15 years younger, but getting fit and losing weight can make you feel 15 years younger, and help you to be a supermodel in your own life. After all, getting your body in shape is all about being the best you can be, not to impress your friends and satisfy your family and/or a partner, but to show yourself that you have the power inside to be who you want to be.

To start, all you have to do is get real about where you are now, take responsibility for your behaviour and, finally, make a plan of action. Better still, this plan is not about starving yourself and sweating it out, but about finding a healthier lifestyle that lasts for life.

Quiz

GET REAL ABOUT YOUR BODY

Becoming conscious of how you think and act when it comes to what you eat and what you do is key when it comes to finding the motivation and willpower to change. No matter how much you think you know about why you're overweight and unfit, the chances are you're missing the bigger picture. The following quiz is designed to give you a clearer insight into your attitude to eating and exercising. Read the questions and go with your gut instinct when answering, then look at the next page for the results.

1. **How much exercise do you take?**
   a. I go to the gym once a week or less. **(D)**
   b. I cycle/walk/gym it for an hour three times a week. **(H)**
   c. I'm not the exercise type. **(EF)**
   d. I'm on my feet all day, I don't need to exercise. **(EE)**

2. **How many meals do you eat in a day?**
   a. Lunch and dinner with snacks. **(EF)**
   b. Breakfast, lunch and dinner with two snacks. **(H)**
   c. One main meal. **(D)**
   d. Three, but I also snack all the time. **(EE)**

3. **How fit are you?**
   a. Fitter than most people. **(H)**
   b. Unfit but that's because I hate exercise. **(EE)**
   c. Unfit but I used to be very fit. **(D)**
   d. It depends on the day. **(EF)**

4. **The reason you can't lose weight is because:**
   a. I eat too much of the wrong foods. **(H)**
   b. Genetics – everyone in my family is fat. **(D)**
   c. Fast food, wine and chocolate. **(EF)**
   d. I eat when I feel unhappy, and I feel unhappy all the time. **(EE)**

5. **Your view of exercise is:**
   a. It's overrated. **(D)**
   b. It's only for the fit. **(EE)**
   c. It's a good weight-loss tool. **(H)**
   d. It's for people with time. **(EF)**

6. **What's your feeling towards fast food?**
   a. I eat it on rare occasions. **(H)**
   b. I know I should resist it, but it tastes great. **(EE)**
   c. Only when I'm starving. **(EF)**
   d. I have a busy life and need to use it. **(D)**

7. **When you run up stairs, how do you feel?**
   a. I feel light-headed. **(EF)**
   b. I feel out of breath. **(EE)**
   c. I can't run, I have to walk. **(D)**
   d. I feel fine. **(H)**

8. **What will it take to make you lose weight?**
   a. A miracle. **(EE)**
   b. More time. **(EF)**
   c. A change of attitude. **(H)**
   d. I will when I decide to. **(D)**

Results

Add up all the answers you gave that were followed by (D) and then those followed by (EF), and so on. Then see which score was the highest. If you scored highest on the (D) answers that makes you Deluded, see below. If you scored highest on the (EF) answers that makes you an Energy Flagger, and so on.

DELUDED (D)

Sorry but you're deluded about why you're overweight and unfit. It sounds harsh but the reality is you're overweight not because of genetics or because you can't be bothered to shed pounds but because you eat too much and do too little. On top of this you don't (or won't) follow healthy food rules: three meals a day and two snacks. To get your body on the healthy track you can't rely on crash diets and miracle diets, you have to eat sensibly, you have to exercise and you have to face up to the fact that the only way to lose weight is to be honest with yourself. That's honest about how you got here and honest about why you're still here. If you can face that then you're halfway to changing your body.

ENERGY FLAGGER (EF)

You're overweight because too much of your food intake comes from junk food, alcohol and snacks. On top of this you're trapped in a vicious circle of erratic eating; wait too long between meals and your blood sugar levels will crash, leading you to pep yourself up with either a stimulant (coffee, diet cola) or a sugar-based snack. This in turn raises your blood sugar level, gives you a small energy high and then causes your sugar levels to crash again, and so on, and so on. This is why you feel tired all the time and can't find the time and space to exercise and eat properly. You need to overhaul your lifestyle so that you can up your energy levels to lose weight and get fit.

HEALTHY (H)

You have a healthy attitude, which means you know how to lose weight and get fit, but it's likely you're not doing it because you can't find your motivation and willpower. Instead of being hard on yourself about your weight, you need to start telling yourself you can do it. 'Stop thinking; start doing' should be your mantra, and put what you know into action. And remember, a fridge full of healthy food is great as long as you eat it, and three times a week at a gym is brilliant but not if you're spending more time on a sun-bed than on the treadmill and/or coming home to eat a post work-out pizza. To lose weight and get in shape, start by re focusing your goals.

EMOTIONAL EATER (EE)

You are what is known as an emotional eater, someone who reaches for food when they feel upset or sad. Maybe you snack when some-one's been mean to you, or reach for chocolate when you feel blue, or just head for the fridge when things go wrong at work. Whatever's driving you, one thing's for sure: in order to lose weight and get fit you need to focus on your emotional demons. Find out why you eat for comfort: is it habit, learnt behaviour or a way to stay overweight and out of the game? Discover your inner workings and you'll be able to drop your weight faster than you ever thought possible.

BODY THERAPY

TAKE RESPONSIBILITY

Let's face it, it's not easy to admit to harsh realties about yourself and take responsibility for where you are today, which is why many of us have a host of excuses about why we can't lose weight and get fit. Maybe you're someone who feels you're overweight because you don't have the time to eat properly, or simply can't afford healthy food. Or maybe you believe that you're different from other people and somehow can't physically lose the kilos (pounds) like they can. You probably also have similar excuses for why you can't or won't exercise, such as 'I'm not the sporty type', 'I don't have the time', and even, 'I can't afford gym membership.'

While all these excuses are valid to some degree, peel away the top layer and you'll find that:

- **If you've got time to eat, you've got time to choose healthy food.**
- **Healthy food is cheaper than takeaway food.**
- **Anyone can lose weight if they eat less and do more.**
- **You don't have to be sporty to be active.**
- **If you've got three hours to watch TV or sit in the pub, you've got 45 minutes to exercise.**
- **You don't need a gym to get fit. You need to get active.**

It's the stories we tell ourselves about our lives that often keep us where we are, and we're all guilty of doing it. However, keep making excuses, and this time next year you'll be in exactly the same place. Of course it's hard to erase excuses when you've been living with them for years, and it's scary to face the world without the comfort of them around you, but if you're determined to change, there's no reason on earth why you can't do it.

One way to find your motivation is to think about how your body and lack of fitness limits your daily life. Does it stop you from trying new things and running about with your kids? Is it making you less confident in a crowd, and more of a doormat with loved ones? More importantly, how will it impact on your future? All it takes is a decision to activate change and get the wheels in motion. I know from my own experience that just the very thought of getting fit and losing weight often left me feeling depressed, fed up and in need of a large bar of chocolate for comfort.

This kind of thinking went on and on until I woke up one day and was just plain fed up with always being the fat one, and I decided that I was going to lose weight. After that enlightening thought, each decision I made rolled into another. Healthy eating led to more energy, which led me to want to exercise. Getting fit led to losing inches (lean muscle takes up three times less space than fat), which meant I started looking leaner, this led to more confidence in myself, which led to more zeal to lose more weight and exercise, and so on, and so on.

STEP ONE:

WARNING – is your body in distress?

Feeling tired and lethargic but don't have the oomph to exercise? Do you know the calorie, fat and carbohydrate value of more than ten foods but still eat the wrong things? If so, you're not alone. Less than 25 per cent of us do the recommended 30 minutes of moderate activity (that's once a day, 5 days a week) and over 75 per cent of us are overweight or obese. Put another way, this means that if you are like the majority of the population, you'd rather sit than go for a walk, and would rather eat something fatty and sugary than reach for an apple.

Back when I was 3 stone (19kg/42lb) overweight my favourite refrain was, 'But I hardly eat anything.' In reality what I meant was I hardly eat anything healthy. Instead I ate a lot of takeaways and snack foods, and drank a lot of alcohol. I'd also say, 'I'm not the exercise type', which translates as 'I am not the exercise type because I have given up before I've even started.'

Weirdly enough, in the end I was the exercise type and healthy eating did work for me because, in between sitting on my sofa and eating crisps and chocolate, I did have more than enough time to buy, cook and eat healthy foods.

My point here is if, like the old me, you keep telling yourself the same old story to excuse your eating, you'll never change because you'll have no reason to.

Clues that it's time to stop making excuses:

- **You're tired all the time, even when you wake up.**
- **You can't remember the last time you ate five portions of fruit and vegetables in one day.**
- **You count walking up the stairs as your daily exercise.**
- **You hope one day you'll wake up thin.**
- **You have bad skin and poor digestion.**
- **You avoid your reflection.**
- **You have no idea how much you eat in a day.**
- **You try every celebrity diet going.**
- **You lie about how much you eat.**
- **You say you'll change tomorrow.**

Of course, we also have amazing ways to validate our position. I used to say the following to make myself feel better:

- **'Being fat is in my genes.'**
- **'I'll get fit when I am not working so hard.'**
- **'I can lose weight, I just don't want to.'**
- **'I know fatter people than me.'**
- **'I'm about 64 kilos (10 stone or 140lb).' (I was closer to 85kg (13 stone or 182lb)!)**

EXERCISE ONE

List three ways to make yourself feel better about your weight and fitness. These could be excuses, comparisons to others, or small white lies you tell yourself.

_____   _____   _____

Now ask yourself:

1. Do these coping mechanisms really make you feel better, or do they have you secretly reaching for the biscuit tin?
2. Excuses and theories aside, what do you think is the one thing holding you back from making a fully formed attempt to lose weight?
3. What would scare you into taking action: a doctor's warning? A plea from a loved one? Or the thought of being like this ten years from now?

STEP TWO:

Find out where your eating habits come from

Food is sustenance, something we eat to fuel our bodies and get us through the day. The problem is food is also a comfort, a treat, something to cheer ourselves up with, something to celebrate over and something to plan our day around. These facts make it hard both to change our view of what we're eating and the way we should eat. In an ideal world we would all have three meals a day and two snacks, but few of us live that life, either because we're too busy or because we just can't change our routines. Instead, we live in a world where we're often stressed and on the run; meaning, food is something that we grab in passing, and the less we have to think about it the better.

This is why to change your eating habits you first have to look at where the habits came from. Do you know what led you to eat the way you do now? Is it learnt behaviour from your family, retaliation for the way someone else tried to get you to eat in the past, or something that you've slowly taught yourself over the years? It may seem pointless to travel back and look at why you eat the way you do, but it's an essential tool in changing your behaviour.

Think back and work out if you have strong memories of how your parents dealt with food, weight and mealtimes. These memories are important because they are the foundations of your eating habits. Maybe you remember one parent using food as a treat, or heard your parents criticising each other's food choices. Or perhaps you lived with a serial yo yo dieter, who existed on cottage cheese and/or someone who policed your eating habits.

Your attitude to food and weight today will be either a replica of one of your parents or a rebellion against their attitude.

To help yourself uncover the past, ask yourself:

- **What positive and negative messages were you given about food and eating when growing up?**
- **When you wanted to eat, how did your parents respond to your request?**
- **Were your parents big eaters or small eaters?**
- **Did your parents have different attitudes to food and weight from each other?**

Looking at how your parents reacted to food highlights messages you hold about food and weight. For example, are you like Jane, 36, who has struggled with the way she eats all her life after learning from her mother that 'Girls should never finish all the food on their plates as men don't like to see women eat.' Or Mandy, 27, who knows the calorie count of more than 100 foods, thanks to living with her parents who were serial yo-yo dieters?

Other possible messages you may have picked up are:

'Girls don't have dessert or second helpings' – Kelly, 29

'It's OK to eat whenever you want' – Sam, 26

'Chocolate helps when you feel down' – Melissa, 32

'Being fat is down to your genes' – Carys, 28

'We're a family who like our food' – Mary, 28

'Only thin girls can do X and Y' – Shannon, 30

EXERCISE TWO

1. Does the way you eat reflect your mother's opinion of food and dieting, your father's style, or neither?
2. List two beliefs you hold about food and exercise.

   a. _____

   b. _____

3. List two beliefs you hold about thin people.

   a. _____

   b. _____

The good thing about body beliefs is that you can change them very quickly. One way to do this is to challenge yourself every time you're about to eat when you're not hungry/eat when you're upset or eat something unhealthy.

1. **Ask yourself how hungry you are.**
2. **If you choose to eat, enjoy what you're eating. Don't just eat it quickly because you feel guilty. Eat it slowly, savour it and chew it.**
3. **Don't feel guilty afterwards. You chose to eat it and you enjoyed the experience, and so you have nothing to feel bad about.**

When it comes to changing your habits for good you need to motivate yourself. Firstly, practise erasing doubt from your voice. Instead of telling yourself why you won't be able to eat healthily, tell yourself why you can do it and keep telling yourself this.

Next, read some motivating 'I did it' weight-loss stories or find a role model who has lost a large amount of weight. Personal accounts from people who have been where you are now can be motivating because they show you that (1) weight loss is a series of small achievable goals not one giant leap; and (2) weight loss is achievable, no matter how big you are.

If you don't believe me, do the following for one week:

1. **Refuse to say you can't do something when it comes to eating healthily.**
2. **Cut out all the junk food, snacks and alcohol, and eat three healthy meals and two snacks a day.**
3. **Each day chart how your body responds to your change in diet and attitude.**
4. **The first two days will be tough, as your body will crave sugar and fat, but after that you'll not only find you feel better (think in terms of mood, sleep and digestion) but also by the end of the week you'll discover more energy and better sleeping patterns, not to mention a weight loss to motivate you to go further.**

STEP THREE:

Fitness – just do it!

Even if you hate, loathe and despise exercise, there's no way around it if you want to get fit and lose weight: you have to be active – not just once a week, but once a day. Before you switch off and stop reading, the good news is that being active and learning to love exercise is not synonymous with being good at it. We're not all made to be natural athletes but we all have the ability to be active and be good at being active. This means that you don't have to run a marathon, win a medal or be the fastest, strongest and most agile to reap the benefits of fitness.

On top of general activity do some exercise five times a week, be it a brisk walk to work, a run round the park or a home workout video, and you'll have something to sing about.

OK, I know what you're thinking: I hate sport/exercise/I have no time/can't be bothered. Were you by any chance a PE loser and the last person picked for teams? If so, this could be why you feel so reluctant to give it a try. Like many a reborn exerciser, I also hated PE lessons and team sports. So much so that once I left school I didn't do a single bit of exercise for ten years believing it wasn't my thing so why should I bother.

Why bother indeed? The facts are clear: exercise is an essential part of life. Apart from the fact that it can help you to lose and maintain your weight loss it also enhances mental health. That is, it gives you a better body image, ups self-esteem and gives you what experts call 'tangible experiences of competency and success': it shows you that you're not hopeless physically, and this in turn leads to better self-confidence. Then again, you may be someone who thinks you're active without doing any exercise. You're on your feet all day or you run up stairs, walk to work – all these things count as activity but they are not the right kind of heart-pounding exercise you need to lose weight. With exercise it's not what you do but how you do it that counts. For example, if you belong to a gym or say you exercise here's what counts:

- **One session a week – this will make you feel as if you're doing something (note the use of the word 'feel').**
- **Two sessions – this will keep your body at a certain level of fitness so that running up stairs won't kill you.**
- **Three sessions – you'll notice your fitness levels increase and weight loss and changes to body shape begin.**
- **Four sessions – is the ideal training frequency. Your fitness levels, strength, muscular development and cardio strength will all improve and body changes will be fast.**

However, there is also no point exercising three or four times a week if you don't raise your pulse above your resting heart rate (that is, there's no point in spending more time in the sauna at the gym, or resting for longer than you work out). To work hard you need to train at 60–75 per cent of your maximum heart rate. The way to work this out is to check if you can speak. If you can speak but find it hard to hold a conversation, you're working at the right intensity.

STEP FOUR:

Give yourself a kick in the pants

Hopefully, by now you know where you're coming from and where you're going. If you're serious about getting into shape, here's the part where you give yourself a huge kick in the pants and ask yourself how have you sabotaged yourself in the past. There comes a point in every fitness plan where you decide, consciously or unconsciously, whether to proceed or give up. If you look back over your past attempts, you may see a pattern to when you gave up.

Was it when you ate a whole packet of biscuits in one go and then thought, 'I've blown it now – so what's the point', or when you reached a small goal and celebrated by giving up (more common than you think)? Perhaps progress was too slow for you and it was easier to just go back to bad habits, or you felt no support from loved ones and so backed down. Maybe you simply got fed up and thought, 'It's not fair that I have to do this', and/or let external issues like work pressure or a family problem stop you in your tracks.

Whatever your reason, it's worth knowing that life doesn't stop being annoying just because you've decided to change. If you're serious about getting into shape and really want to do it, you have to play with the cards you've been dealt; that is, do it even though you're time starved/stressed/under pressure and bored by the very thought of it.

EXERCISE FOUR

1. Ask yourself: if you carry on the way you are now, what would your future worst-case scenario be?
2. Now write down three things you'd like to do but don't do because of your weight and lack of fitness. This can be anything from joining a gym, going dancing, to having a baby or finding a partner.

   a. _____

   b. _____

   c. _____

3. How will you feel in five years if you still haven't done these things?
4. What is your number-one reason for wanting to change?

The aim of the above is not to have you running back to the biscuit tin but to try to get you to see that what you do today has serious consequences on how you'll live tomorrow. By attaching a painful picture of the future to what you're doing today you can find the extra motivation you need to change. The next step is to find your future goals. By using the above exercise as motivation, work out what your specific goals will be for the next month, six months and a year.

Help yourself by:

1. Writing three changes you'd like to make to your body in a month, six months and a year.

   a. _____

   b. _____

   c. _____

2. Make these changes attainable; that is, don't wish to lose 3 stone (19kg/42lb) in a month. Also, be specific, don't just say, 'I want to lose weight', but 'I want to lose 6 kilos (12lb) in a month.'

3. Put your goals in the present tense and write them down. Be specific, don't say, 'I want to stop eating junk', but 'I will throw out all junk food on Monday and shop for healthy food.'

4. Now place your goals where you can see them. You'll have a higher chance of reaching your goals if you keep them always at the front of your mind.

BODY REHAB
GETTING FIT THE HEALTHY WAY

Whereas dieting is out because it literally makes you want to eat all the foods you desire or encourages you to cut out whole food groups and/or starve yourself, the one fact you do have to come to terms with when trying to lose weight is: CALORIES COUNT. This doesn't mean count your calories, but watch how much you eat.

Your aim should be to:

1. Practise portion control.

2. Cut back on snacking and junk food.

3. Make healthier food choices when you're out.

4. Eat five portions of fruit and vegetables a day.

5. Eat less of what you know makes you fat.

6. Change your life so that you're not tempted by old food choices.

7. Cook more meals and buy less ready-made ones.

8. Experiment with unknown foods.

9. Cut down on alcohol and full-fat lattes.

10. Do some exercise.

THE RULES

BODY FREEDOM – LOSING WEIGHT AND GETTING FIT

Temporary starvation, also known as dieting, is bad news for your body, whereas eating regular healthy meals with two healthy snacks a day, combined with regular exercise, is the way to the new trim you – and it will ensure you stay that way.

DON'T SKIP MEALS

Skipping meals is bad news for the body's metabolism because after four hours without food the body will suppress its ability to burn calories. Drastically cut your calorie input further with a crash diet and your body will reduce its calorie-burning potential by as much as 30 per cent. Your metabolism rises when you eat, as the body needs to burn energy for digesting and absorbing food – so eat more frequently.

CUT OUT ALCOHOL

Alcohol is full of calories and empty ones at that – they give you no nutrients and no vitamins. If you stick to a healthy diet but regularly down pints or glasses of wine a night your weight loss is going to be negligible.

If you can't say no, remember the rule: don't drink anything alcoholic you can't see through (the clearer the drink – for example vodka and gin - the less calories compared to cream liqueurs and pints).

THINK MORE PROTEIN AND LESS CARBOHYDRATE

Focus on protein to stoke your fat-burning fires. Not only is it harder to digest and so uses 20–30 per cent more energy for digestion (an extra 150 to 200 calories a day) but it also forces your metabolic rate upwards. Mix it with good carbohydrates, such as green leafy vegetables and fruit, as it's this combination that will dramatically change the way your body burns calories.

GO SLOW ON FAST FOOD

Burgers, pizza, chips, kebabs, chicken nuggets, fried chicken, and fish and chips – it all counts as junk food. This is the type of food that most people who need to get fit dine out on. If this is you, it's likely you do it because (1) it's cheap; and (2) it tastes good. The bad news is it tastes good because it's loaded with fat and sugar; it's also calorie dense and guaranteed to make you fat if you eat it more than once a week. Sadly, if you're trying to get fit, it's this kind of food that you have to cut down on.

SAY NO TO FATTY SNACKS

Crisps, chocolate bars, sweets, muffins, savoury snacks, cereal bars, flapjacks and brownies – these are just some of the foods you may be choosing to snack on, which is bad news for your body as they are heavy in calories and rich in fat and sugar. Snack healthily by opting for one of the following: oatcakes, a handful of nuts, a piece of fruit, dried fruit, or a smoothie.

GET TO GRIPS WITH FAT

A diet high in saturated fat (fat that's hard at room temperature – think butter and cheese), can lead to heart disease and weight gain, and the bad news is that fat is often hidden in foods, as it is the very thing that makes food taste good. Foods with saturated fat also do not help to fill you up. For example, a large jacket potato has less calories and less fat than a bag of cheese and onion crisps and keeps you fuller for longer.

BE ACTIVE

Do 20–40 minutes of vigorous aerobic exercise four to five times a week, making sure your heart is working at the right intensity. Exercise studies show that the intensity of effort required for effective health benefits means you need to aim for at least 60–75 per cent of your Age Predicted Maximum Heart Rate (APMHR). To find this, take your age and subtract it from 220. This means that if you are 25 years old, your APMHR is 195 and you should be working at around 120, as seen below.

TRAINING ZONE

Age	AMPHR	60–75%
20	200	120–150
25	195	117–146
30	190	114–142

If you don't have a heart monitor, then think about how you feel. Too breathless to talk? You're likely to be right where you want to be.

GETTING STARTED

BEING REALISTIC ABOUT YOUR GOALS

Organising yourself before you start on your new healthy lifestyle will make you more likely to succeed. You will also feel in control and positive – this is not about denying yourself all the good things in life, it's more about allowing you to enjoy the best things in life and feeling better for it.

1. Make a plan

To ensure you reach your goals, make a plan; without one your journey to lose weight and get fit will be a bit like going on a journey without a map or vehicle. It's good to be motivated; however, attacking your life with zest is one thing, but changing your life too radically means a fast burn-out and a return to old habits.

The key is to set goals that are ambitious but attainable for you. It's hard to do this when you've got a picture in your mind about where you would like to be or a vague idea of where you are now, so start armed with the following information.

Get yourself a journal/book of blank paper. This is going to be your food and fitness diary. Studies show that people who write things down are more likely to reach their goals because they continually remind themselves of where they are now, and where they are going.

So, starting with today's date, write down your:

Weight _____

Waist measurement _____

Bust measurement _____

Hip measurement _____

Dress size _____

If you don't want to weigh yourself, go by your clothing measurement. The aim here is not to adhere to a weight chart but to give yourself a figure by which to compare your future successes by. If you can't bear to measure yourself or write your dress size down, put a recent photograph of yourself (one you dislike) into your book.

Now flick 30 pages ahead in your book and think of where you'd like to be in a month's time and write that down. Be realistic – you can make a big difference in a month; a good aim is to lose 1–1.5 kilos (2–3lb) a week but you're not going to drop 30kg (66lb) miraculously in four weeks – even if you have a lot of weight to lose, though you should lose more than 2kg a week to begin with. The more weight you have to lose the faster your weight loss and vice versa.

Future weight _____

Future waist measurement _____

Future bust measurement _____

Future hip measurement _____

Future dress size _____

Now go back to your start page and write down a goal for every day of your first week. A day goal can be anything from:
• **Throwing out all the junk food in your cupboards.**
• **Joining a gym.**
• **Going for a brisk walk.**

- **Eating five portions of fruit and vegetables.**
- **Drinking eight glasses of water.**
- **Having a healthy lunch.**

Now, think of an end-of-week goal. This can be anything from:
- **Exercising for 30 minutes every single day.**
- **Eating proper meals and healthy snacks every day.**
- **Saying no to takeaway food for a whole week.**
- **Avoiding a treat mentality every single day.**
- **Weaning yourself off chocolate or alcohol.**
- **Losing a kilo or more.**

Finally, think of your month goal. This should be something like:
- **Lose 4–6kg (9–14lb).**
- **Fit into a smaller dress size.**
- **Wear an article of clothing you've never been able to get into.**
- **Run 2 km (1 $^1/_4$ miles) without passing out.**
- **Feel good about yourself.**

2. Create a calorie deficit

To lose weight effectively you need to create a calorie deficit by either reducing your calorie intake (eating less) or by increasing the amount of calories you burn (through exercise), but by far the fastest way is to ensure you do both. To lose 0.5kg (1lb) of body fat, all you need to do is reduce your food intake or up your exercise intake by 3,500 calories a week. That's 500 calories a day.

Research shows that if you aim to lose 10 per cent of your body weight you are more likely to do it and keep the weight off. So the next step in creating your plan is to find yourself an eating plan that works for you. That's a plan that takes a little bit of what you like, and erases all the rest. The aim in a nutshell is to stop eating processed ready-made food, and start eating healthy foods. Stop snacking on sugar-laden products and start eating more fruit and vegetables.

However, to get here you have to incorporate healthy eating, not dieting, into your mind. If healthy eating conjures up all the things you don't like to eat, it's time to give new foods a chance. If you can't do this, remind yourself of your number-one goal: TO LOSE WEIGHT!

The reality is that none of us are made to be overweight. Less than 1 per cent of us are genetically made to be fat, we get fat through bad lifestyle choices. To help yourself, pick up your fitness journal and start keeping a food diary that ensures you eat a diet that's made up of:

• **50 per cent carbohydrates – vegetables, fruit and unrefined carbs like brown rice and wholemeal bread.**
• **25 per cent protein – lean meat, fish, eggs, soya protein, pulses.**
• **25 per cent unsaturated fats – nuts, seeds, oily fish.**

Here's what you should be eating every day:

CARBOHYDRATES

Foods known as carbohydrates are divided into refined (products that have had all the goodness taken out of them in the milling process) and unrefined (products that still have the kernel of grain within them). For a healthy diet you need to eat more unrefined carbohydrates because these are the ones converted to energy and not stored directly as fat.

FRUIT AND VEGETABLES – FIVE PORTIONS A DAY

Apples, bananas and green leafy vegetables are particularly good as they are crammed full of vitamins and minerals and also add fibre to your diet. A portion in the five-a-day rule is approximately 80g (3oz), equivalent to a medium apple or banana, and two to three table-spoons of vegetables (raw, cooked, frozen or canned). No matter how much 100 per cent fruit juice you drink, it still represents only one portion towards the five-a-day target.

PROTEIN

Protein is essential because, unlike fat, 1g of protein has less than 4 calories, whereas 1g of fat has 9 calories. A diet rich in protein (as opposed to protein-only diets) will also control your appetite and stimulate your hormones to burn fat in the body. Protein-only diets do have their benefits, but, like any diet, they are tough to stick to and don't teach you to eat healthily.

UNSATURATED FAT

Olive oil, salmon, tuna and sardines, nuts and seeds contain essential fatty acids, also known as unsaturated fat (fat that is liquid at room temperature, such as olive oil). This is good for your heart health, hair, skin and weight loss, which is why oily fish, which are rich in omega-3 essential fatty acids, should be added to your diet three times a week for maximum benefits (vegetarians can eat a small amount of walnuts to get their omega-3). Eat small amounts of nuts and seeds to obtain the other essential fatty acid, omega-6.

3. Listen to your body

Your body knows what it needs on the healthy food front even if you keep doing otherwise. If you want one more reason to take hold of your diet, look at your symptoms to see where you're going wrong with food:

Problem	**Feeling bloated – it's likely you eat too many wheat-based products.**
Solution	**Make sure you up your fibre intake. Eat more vegetables over pasta and stick to non-wheat breads, such as rye.**
Problem	**Feeling tired – too much sugar can make your blood sugar levels surge, causing a mood high followed by a dip in energy, and irritability.**
Solution	**Don't skip meals and then look for quick fixes. Eat every three to four hours and snack on fruit, not chocolate.**
Problem	**Feeling constipated.**
Solution	**You need more fibre and more water. Your body needs fluid to help waste matter exit the body. Aim for eight glasses a day.**
Problem	**You're in dire need of the bathroom.**
Solution	**Too much sugar in your diet causes diarrhoea. Cut back by reading food labels to see how much sugar you're consuming.**
Problem	**You crave sweet things – you are 'addicted' to sugar.**
Solution	**Detox by cutting out all sugar for a week and reintroduce it slowly using natural sugars only, such as fruit.**
Problem	**You're gaining weight even though you're cutting back.**
Solution	**Look at your portion sizes.**

HIDDEN CALORIES

- Fast food – high in hidden salts, fat and sugars, not to mention calories.
- Snacks – high in sugar and fat, and often calorie loaded.
- Takeaway coffees – lattes are loaded with full-fat milk, and grande and vente sizes sometimes contain as much as 450ml ($^3/_4$ pint) of full-fat milk.
- Fizzy drinks – loaded with sugar (sometimes 13 spoons per can).
- Processed ready-made meals – high in calories, sugar and salt.

Problem   **You can't sleep.**

Solution   **Eat earlier – late-night takeaways mean late-night digestion. Also avoid caffeine (a strong stimulant) after 4.00 p.m., earlier if you are a fizzy cola and café latte junkie, as caffeine needs plenty of time to exit the body.**

Problem   **You have cellulite.**

Solution   **Cellulite is just another name for fat and, as it's impossible to spot reduce (that is, lose fat from just one area), you need to maintain a healthy diet that concentrates on all-over weight loss.**

4. Get sweaty

The aim is to make exercising part of your everyday routine, you'll be more likely to stick to it, and part of doing this is to consider what type of exercise works for you.

Firstly, it's important to get aerobic. Aerobic exercise is running, swimming, walking (briskly) and cycling. This is the type of exercise that takes effort and exertion and so requires lots of oxygen, breathing and heart-pumping work. To work out if you're doing it correctly, you should always exercise to a level where you can speak, but wouldn't be able to hold a whole conversation.

Alongside aerobic exercise you need to ensure that you do strengthening work. This is the type of exercise that helps make you look lean. This happens because muscle is an active tissue (unlike fat which does nothing but make you look big), so it basically eats up energy in your body. This means the more overall muscle you have, the more calories you will burn (meaning, you can eat more food and not gain weight, or eat more healthily and lose weight). Strength training is work with free weights, martial arts, yoga and Pilates.

If you want to get into the exercise habit, then the obvious option is to go for something you'll enjoy and therefore will want to do, so find a form of exercise that fits in with your daily habits. For example:

WALKING

Good for beginners and people who hate gyms.
This is cheap, easy to do and, according to the British Heart Foundation, all it takes to stay fit is just 10,000 steps a day. Walking your way to health works because walking not only improves the cardiovascular system (the lungs and heart) but also increases your strength and tones your muscles.

RUNNING

Good for weight loss and competitive people.
Running needs a high level of exertion, and so requires a lot of oxygen, breathing and heart-pumping work. This is essential for fitness, as it lowers your risk of a serious disease, burns body fat and generally keeps you fit, and looking trim. Running is also a huge calorie burner as you can burn nearly 500 calories in just 45 minutes.

SWIMMING

Good if you have a lot of weight to lose and you want to exercise alone.
Swimming properly (that's swimming without stopping for five minutes at each end) improves upper- and lower-body strength as well as aerobic strength. It's also cheap and can be easily done at your local pool.

CYCLING

Good if you want to trim your lower body and be outside.
As tempting as it is, don't rely on momentum to get you around. This is where you sail down hills, and let the gradient do all the work for you. The aim with cycling is to put in some effort, so go at a steady pace, and challenge yourself with some hills to get cardiovascular benefit.

Once you've chosen your pursuits your aim should be to do one for 30 minutes every day, so start by getting off the sofa. Remember: if you've got time to surf eBay and watch the soaps on TV, you have time to exercise. The key is time-management. Cut back on a sedentary pursuit (an activity where you're sitting on your bottom and not moving) in favour of an active one, and don't give up. Back in the early days of exercising, like many beginners I would spend more time debating whether or not I should go out and do some exercise than knuckling down and getting it over with. So it helps to know that your first few attempts will probably feel like a struggle while your mind battles with a million reasons why you shouldn't do it. The good news is: research shows you have to do something ten times in order to make it a habit and that means by this time next week you will be well on your way to being an exerciser.

TEN WAYS TO FIND THE TIME TO EXERCISE

(aim for more than the recommended minimum of 30 minutes a day if you want is to lose weight)

1. Get up an hour earlier.

2. Do two 30-minute segments each day.

3. Do it in your lunch hour.

4. Do it at weekends.

5. Forgo something else you regularly do.

6. Exercise with friends instead of going out to the cinema.

7. Watch less TV (most people watch four hours a night).

8. Walk to work instead of driving/taking transport.

9. Plan ahead so that you can make time.

10. Make it a daily essential, like brushing your teeth.

5. Make your new lifestyle work for you

Also known as: don't try to live with a foot in both worlds. Yes, you can afford to have a small daily treat such as a chocolate bar, but you can't afford to have a huge blow-out once a day and be super-strict the next. The idea is to make your new plan the only plan you follow (let's face it, the last one didn't work so well for you, so what have you got to lose?) and the only way to do this is to be committed to your goals. Help yourself make your lifestyle work:

GIVE YOURSELF A MONTH TO GET USED TO IT

It probably took you around ten years or more to gain the weight and fitness level you're currently at, so you're not going to change your ways overnight. Give your plan a chance by working out your weak spots and making sure you bypass them. For Jasmine, 29, it's:

'Friday night in the pub. I can be good all week but once I am out with my boyfriend and friends, I end up drinking till I am drunk and then having a kebab on the way home.'

Whatever your weak spot, be it the 4.00 p.m. chocolate bar, the large latte at breakfast or the midnight kebab, change your habits to fit in with your new plan.

FIND A CHEERLEADER

If you really can't do it on your own, think about getting a fitness expert to help. Not only can they get you through the rough moments but they can also help push you further when the going gets tough. Better still, find yourself a get-fit buddy – a friend who will encourage you to work harder and longer when you're exercising, and help you to stick to your healthy food regime. Choose someone who you view as encouraging, not someone who will bring you your favourite foods on the side, and give you excuses to have a day off from working out.

DON'T STEREOTYPE YOURSELF

If you have a bad day, put it down to just that, and move on – don't give up. Just because you have tried and failed before doesn't mean that you will fail this time. By putting doubt into your head and saying, 'I can't do this', 'I'm useless at sport/dieting', 'I have no willpower', you are closing yourself off to succeeding. Instead, grab a challenge and do something outside of your usual box; it will help to motivate you to keep going. Try taking up a new sport, try something new on the food front each day, learn to cook, go organic – do anything that allows you into new opportunities, and don't allow others (or yourself) to label you. Prove them wrong.

TOUGH IT OUT

Let's be honest, there will be days and times when the plan gets hard. Maybe external forces will have you craving a drink or a chocolate bar, or internal forces will just make you feel like giving up because it feels easier to do that than go on. When that happens you have to make yourself tough it out. One way to do this is to get away from temptation. Grab your keys, leave your purse behind and go for a long walk. If you can't do that, run a bath and make yourself lie in it for 15 minutes. Too time-starved? Then turn the radio up and dance madly around your kitchen for five minutes. The idea is to break your thought pattern and, instead of focusing on having a chocolate biscuit, immediately make yourself think of something else. If you do cave in and succumb, it's not the end of the world. Don't use it as an excuse to give up totally, instead just carry on. It's what you do in the long term that counts more.

6. A word about weight and coupledom

When you're in love it seems like nothing else matters, including your diet, which is why studies show falling in love can help you to gain 4.5kg (10lb) in a year. Part of the problem is that when you're dating much of your socialising occurs around food and drink, so the chances are you slowly start upping your calorie intake without even noticing. By the time you do notice, it's too late because you've gained weight. The good news is love and weight gain go hand in hand only if you let them. Help yourself by:

1. Being sure not to match your partner's meal portion for portion. Men are bigger and need more calories, so your serving should always be a third smaller than his.
2. If you're in conflict over food and weight, discuss the attitudes and advice you both grew up with around food and weight, and see if you can find a healthy living pattern that suits you both.
3. Don't let your partner police your meals or your weight (and don't police his) – it's a recipe for arguments and fights.
4. Work out together – studies show couples who sweat together, stay together.
5. Don't cook separate meals – it's too much of a temptation to you.
6. If he's sabotaging your efforts, confront him and ask him what he's really worried about.
7. Lose weight and get fit for yourself not for someone else.
8. If he needs to lose weight, too, suggest going on an exercise and healthy eating plan together.

One-month Body Makeover

The aim of the one-month planner is to take a step-by-step approach to changing your body. Incorporate each tip into your daily life until it becomes second nature. The three body rules are:

1. **Exercise every day for 30 minutes minimum.**

2. **Eat three healthy meals and two snacks a day.**

3. **Write in your body journal every day.**

> I always loathed and hated PE at school, but at the age of 29 I forced myself to join a gym to lose weight and was surprised to find that it's really good fun. Apart from losing weight, I just love the feeling of getting stronger both inside and out and of being able to do something I always thought was beyond my capabilities.
>
> **SAM, 32**

WEEK ONE

MONDAY

Work out your long- and short-term goals (see Body Rehab) and write them down in a journal. Use this to chart your successes daily. Then take action by (1) ditching all the junk food in your cupboards; and (2) going for a brisk 30-minute walk after dinner and lunch (do this every day if you're not doing any other exercise).

TUESDAY

Start eating three healthy meals and two snacks a day. No alcohol and no junk food, and round it off by doing a healthy food shop so that you can plan and organise your meals.

WEDNESDAY

Treat exercise as if it were as important as going to work – it helps to you to avoid the temptation to not do it. Then find the telephone number of your local gym or swimming pool and buy a home workout video so that you have no excuse not to do something every day.

THURSDAY

Try at least two new healthy foods today, and then cook a dinner that contains at least four types of vegetables (not potatoes) and a portion of protein. Your aim should be to eat five portions of fruit and vegetables a day.

FRIDAY

Make a list of the people, places and items you think most influence you to give up on a weight loss and exercise plan. Come up with three ways to resist each temptation.

SATURDAY

Declutter your wardrobe to prepare for the new and improved you. Throw away anything that reminds you of who you used to be. Large hold-me-in knickers and 'fat' clothes need to be dumped. Then inspire yourself by focusing on how you'd like to look in a month.

SUNDAY

How raw is your food? Food in its natural state is best, so detox for a day and eat raw vegetables, salads, fruit and nuts. Drink pure juices and herbal teas. It will clear your system out for the week.

WEEK TWO

MONDAY
Make breakfast, lunch and dinner every day this week and do as much of it in advance a possible to get used to preparing for your meals and finding the time to cook even when you're busy.

TUESDAY
Do a big grocery shop and read all the food labels to see what you're eating. Go for fresh and raw over processed and ready made.

WEDNESDAY
Eat five portions of fruit and vegetables a day, every day.

THURSDAY
Cancel any night out that will tempt you to break your healthy eating plan this week. Focus on a future event (birthday/wedding/holiday) to inspire you to forgo the present for the sake of the future.

FRIDAY
Look at your exercise diary – are you doing enough and at the right intensity? Has your fitness improved? If not you need to work harder or try something different.

SATURDAY
Do your clothes feel looser? After two weeks you should be noticing a difference. Check your diary for your start figures and work out your progress. If you've lost your target amount of weight allow yourself one treat.

SUNDAY
Stockpile healthy meals. Spend all day knocking up healthy dishes and freeze them or leave them in the fridge, so that you have fast healthy food on hand when you're hungry.

WEEK THREE

MONDAY
Set yourself a new exercise goal, such as running every day for 30 minutes for the next two weeks, or a 10km (6 mile) run in three months, or to learn boxing/salsa, or be able to do 20 press-ups without stopping. Work towards this goal from now on.

TUESDAY
Get used to knowing what you're eating for snacks. If the food label is as long as your arm, don't eat that snack. Instead, think raw and natural. Eat nuts (raw and unsalted), fruit, seed bars (not flapjack or 'healthy' bars that contain sugars.

WEDNESDAY
Work out ways you can lose weight faster. Are you drinking extra calories in fruit juices? If so, dilute half a glass with water. Are takeaway coffees adding up the calories? If so, always ask for a skinny (coffee with skimmed milk). Are you eating refined carbohydrates (white bread, rice and pasta)? If so, stick to wholegrain/wholemeal varieties that have more fibre and less sugar.

THURSDAY
Think about your water habit. Firstly, make sure you drink the required eight glasses of water a day. This aids digestion, stops hunger and helps you avoid snacking. Secondly, make sure you don't drink extra calories in terms of fizzy drinks and alcohol. Both are high in sugar and have no nutrients.

FRIDAY
Change your social habits for good. In order to make healthy living a new way of life, you have to cut out all your unhealthy habits, such as midnight takeaways, weekend fry-ups and scoffing a bag of family-sized sweets at the cinema. To help yourself, take snacks to the cinema, get used to eating no later than 8.00 p.m. and grill your fry-ups!

SATURDAY
Ask your friends' advice on how they think you should make the most of yourself. Then go shopping for new clothes that will change your image.

SUNDAY
Check your progress and evaluate what's working for you and what's not. Check your diary and work out what you need to change and what you need to do more of.

WEEK FOUR

MONDAY

Open your mind to new possibilities – now that you're feeling healthier, what other goals can you incorporate into your life to boost your confidence and your esteem? A new job? A new relationship? Even a new hairstyle?

TUESDAY

Get naked and really look at your body in the mirror. Instead of being critical, see if you can notice the difference in weight loss, skin tone and muscle improvement. What areas would you particularly like to firm up and how are you going to do it?

WEDNESDAY

Work out who's on your team. You're nearly a month into your new plan – who's been helpful and who hasn't? Who can you rely on to encourage you onward? These are the people to hang around with and make new plans with.

THURSDAY

Write down in your journal how eating healthily and being active has made you feel. Opt for ten improvements in your overall everyday life.

FRIDAY

Have a blow-out night – you've nearly made it to a month, go out and celebrate but keep your alcohol and food intake in check; that is, don't overdo it or your body will pay you back tomorrow.

SATURDAY

You should be in the swing of things by now, so plan a trip for the summer and set yourself a new body goal for it.

SUNDAY

Check your progress via your clothes, or weighing scales and see how far you've come. No matter how well you've done, remember to stay watchful of what's happening and don't fall back into old habits. Celebrate by all means, but set new goals for the next month first.

Career

Introduction

Are you dreaming of a job that brings you wealth, fame and instant gratification, or one that has ten weeks' holiday a year and no stress attached? Or maybe you're slowly boring yourself to death in a dead-end job, knowing in your heart that you can do more and are worth more than this? Or perhaps you're one of the many who are desperately waiting for inspiration to hit and your perfect made-to-measure job to pop into your head.

Wherever you're at, one thing is for sure, most of us simply don't bother to think about our working life, until something goes wrong with it. This means if your job is currently on your mind, the chances are that money, boredom, a feeling of going nowhere fast, and/or something outside of your control (a redundancy, evil boss or an office move) has pushed you to consider where you're going in your life, and why. Of course, this in itself brings problems, as finding a new career or direction isn't easy, especially if you're fearful of starting again, losing a monthly wage or retraining. It's also tough if you're stuck at the first hurdle and unaware of your skills, and oblivious to what interests you in life. If any or all of the above sound familiar, you're not alone. The number-one problem most people have with their jobs is not knowing what they want to do or what they're good at, which is why most people end up in jobs they are only mildly interested in.

'Easy for you to say', friends often gripe, simply because I happened to be one of the people who did know what I wanted. However, the point my friends are missing is this: I wasn't born to be a writer and had never felt a driving need to be a writer. I simply decided that writing was what I liked doing and so that's what I was going to do. So, if you feel stuck, this is the point to start from: what do you like? What do you love doing, and what makes you happy? It may not point immediately to a job or career (more of that later), but knowing what you enjoy will give you an indication of what you should be searching for in a job.

The fact is you will spend five days a week over approximately 40 years of your life working, and so you deserve to have a job that makes you feel good, competent and happy. Too much to ask for, you may be thinking — well not really. The perfect job for you is the job that keeps you fulfilled, because at the end of the day job satisfaction is what it's all about. This doesn't mean you have to be a career type or a high flyer but it does mean that you have to be willing to work at finding the right job for you, because, like your finances and your relationships, you have to go through a practical thought process in order to discover the new successful you!

Quiz

WHAT'S YOUR CAREER POTENTIAL?

Think you're hard-working? Practical? A team player? Knowing yourself inside and out is key when it comes to finding your ideal job. The following quiz is designed to give you a clearer insight into your attitude about work. Go with your gut feeling when answering then look at the next page for the results.

1. **How did you get into your current career?**
   a. By blagging your way in. **(P)**
   b. You saw it advertised and thought: why not? **(DR)**
   c. A friend/contact got you in, but it's definitely not your dream job. **(D)**
   d. You needed money. **(R)**

2. **A big project with a fast turnaround comes up at work. Do you:**
   a. Pray you don't have to work on it? **(R)**
   b. Ask if you can be a team leader? **(P)**
   c. Keep your head down when they ask for volunteers. **(DR)**
   d. Wish you didn't have to be on the team? **(D)**

3. **You have to give a presentation. Do you feel:**
   a. Sick with nerves, as you hate being in the limelight? **(DR)**
   b. Eager to go for it and show what you can do? **(P)**
   c. You're wasted doing this stuff? **(D)**
   d. It's a complete waste of time? **(R)**

4. **The reason you feel frustrated at work is because:**
   a. You hate working. **(R)**
   b. You are undervalued. **(P)**
   c. You'd rather be doing something completely different. **(D)**
   d. You have no idea why you're there. **(DR)**

5. **Your dream job is offered to you. How do you feel?**
   a. Happy – you knew this would happen one day. **(D)**
   b. Surprised – you had no idea this would happen. **(DR)**
   c. Worried – it sounds too good to be true. **(R)**
   d. Vindicated – all the hard work was worth it. **(P)**

6. **Finish this sentence: I work . . .**
   a. … to live. **(DR)**
   b. … because I like it. **(P)**
   c. … because I can't get into the job I want. **(D)**
   d. … because I have to. **(R)**

7. **What's your biggest work skill?**
   a. You're an organised team player. **(P)**
   b. You work hard. **(DR)**
   c. You're honest. **(R)**
   d. You know what you would like to be doing. **(D)**

8. **Would you do more training to get your ideal job?**
   a. No, you're too old and it wouldn't help anyway. **(R)**
   b. Yes, it's always worth getting more skills. **(P)**
   c. Yes, if your firm paid you to do it. **(DR)**
   d. No, because what you want takes natural talent. **(D)**

Results

Add up all the answers you gave that were followed by (D) and then those followed by (P), and so on. Then see which score was the highest. If you scored highest on the (D) answers that makes you a Dreamer, see below. If you scored highest on the (P) answers that makes you a Planner, and so on.

DREAMER (D)

When it comes to a career, it's good to have dreams. They help you to see where you want to be and tend to help you focus. However, the problem is that if you just focus on the outcome and don't look at the details, dreams tend to stay daydreams and never become a reality. So ask yourself what are you doing to get from where you are now to where you want to be. Very few people get plucked from obscurity and offered their dream on a plate. Meaning, it takes graft, perseverance and discipline to get to where you want to be. If you're stuck in a job that pays the bills but isn't what you want, you need to work out ways to gather more skills and get closer to your dream.

PLANNER (P)

You're a planner who does all the right things to make inroads and get yourself up the career ladder. However, if you're currently feeling frustrated and/or stuck, it's probably because you're not reaching your full potential. If you're happy with your career, the chances are it's your current job that's not right. This means it's time to think outside the box. Consider how you could make your job work for you in different fields, or if you could be self-employed, or even if you can take your current skills and mix and match them into a completely new job.

DRIFTER (DR)

Drifters do as the name implies: they drift into a job and work hard at it, never really considering if they might be good at something else. The chances are you live for your evenings and your weekends and really have no idea what you want to do workwise or what you're good at, probably because you have never given yourself the time and space to think about it. If so, it's time to consider that your social life and leisure pursuits may be good indicators of a potential career for you. Remember: work has the power to be satisfying and fun as long as you put the effort in to find out what it is you want.

REJECTOR (R)

You're a rejector; someone who rejects the idea of job satisfaction before they have even thought about it. The chances are you rarely get promoted and your colleagues often accuse you of being negative when new ideas and schemes come up. Maybe this is due to disappointment in the past, frustration in the present or setbacks in your working life. Or maybe you just don't believe work can be an enjoyable experience, and so what's the point in trying? If you feel like this, it's time for a change of mindset. Give it a go; after all, what have you got to lose?

CAREER THERAPY

WORK TO LIVE, OR LIVE TO WORK?

If you dread Sunday nights, live it up at weekends and are out most week nights, I would say you probably fall into the work-to-live side of working. On the other hand, if you graft every day and do overtime quite happily in pursuit of the greater picture, then it's likely you live to work. Whatever your take on the working life, if you're reading this chapter the chances are you're either looking for a new direction or have been forced to re-evaluate your work goals.

Of course, it may feel like the end of the world when you realise the time has come to change jobs and maybe even careers; I know, because I've been there. Fourteen years ago I had my perfect job. This was the job I'd been dreaming about since I was 14 years old. It paid well, it won me prizes and had fantastic kudos. Plus, I got to work with an amazing team of people who were fun to be around, and I got to travel abroad. The only problem was that after three years I hated it. At first I put it down to a passing phase, but when that passing phase turned into a year, I thought I needed a new direction and so got a promotion. After a year of that, the dread slowly returned, so I applied for new jobs, thinking I needed a new challenge, but the only problem was the moment I was offered a new job I knew I didn't want it.

This eventually led me to the possible revelation that maybe the job I had wanted all my life and worked towards perhaps wasn't the right job for me after all. I was ready to throw it all in when a clever friend pointed out that maybe I was taking a sledgehammer approach to a more fragile problem. Her theory was that maybe I didn't hate my career but I hated only my job but was so stuck into it that I couldn't see the wood for the trees. For me, this was a light-bulb moment, because when I stopped moaning loudly about how frustrated, bored and miserable I was, I realised that the things I was frustrated with were being stuck in an office all day and being told to write things I no longer found challenging. The solution, therefore, as my clever friend had predicted, was not to give up on my career but to approach the problem from a different perspective. So I went freelance and never looked back.

My point here is that job satisfaction is not just about finding your perfect job. Being happy in a job/career is an ongoing process that requires you to pay constant attention to where you're going and why. This is because your career isn't something separate from your life, it's a major part of your life that will change and expand as you do. Meaning, what's right for you today may not be right for you tomorrow, but that doesn't mean you made the wrong decision, but that you need to make another one.

STEP ONE:

WARNING – it pays to know yourself

The key to a successful and happy work life is to ensure that what you do for a living is in synch with who you are. Of course, this is all well and good if you know what you're good at and what makes you happy. But, unfortunately, most of us don't take the time out to give this ample thought, and so usually fall into any old job we're offered and rarely consider if we can do more or not.

Clues that it's time to think about your career include:

- **Taking 'sickie' days because you're totally fed up.**
- **Moaning about your job daily.**
- **Feeling frustrated when you arrive at work.**
- **Feeling bored by lunchtime.**
- **Spending more time emailing friends than working.**
- **Feeling disheartened when you think you'll be doing this every day until you retire.**
- **Living for your holidays and weekends.**
- **Wanting more money, better prospects and more job satisfaction.**

It's scary to admit you're unfulfilled and unhappy, but ultimately worth it because there's nothing more demoralising than sitting day in and day out in a job that sucks away all your confidence. This means, if you're on the lookout for a career change, your first challenge is to step back from your life and give yourself some time to ask yourself the following question and consider your response:

'What do I want to do, and why?'

Possible answers:
- **'I don't know.'**
- **'Make loads of money.'**
- **'Be famous.'**
- **'Have a job with no stress.'**
- **'Get loads of holiday.'**
- **'Not work.'**

The above are some of the common responses to that question, and if one of them is yours, it might help to know that you are on the right track as long as you consider your response, and not see it as a dead-end statement. For example:

65

'I don't know'

All this means is that at the moment you don't know what you want to do because you haven't given it enough practical thought. See the exercises on the following pages.

'Make loads of money'

If this is your motivation, you should be looking for jobs that reap high financial rewards and bonuses, such as trading, banking and being self-employed.

'Be famous'

What do you want to be famous for? Once you know, you can learn or hone that skill and push it to the maximum.

'Have a job with no stress'

This is unlikely but not impossible. Think about what makes you feel stressed at work (pressure to hit targets, deadlines) and think of jobs that don't contain these elements.

'Get loads of holiday'

Think about teaching (ten weeks holiday a year), being self-employed (time off whenever you want), jobs in the holiday industry.

'Not work'

You need to be realistic. Even rich people work because they know they can't aimlessly wander through days. Opt for careers that give you more freedom, i.e. freelancing, self-employment.

EXERCISE ONE

To focus on what makes you tick, answer the following questions. Take your time, because these questions are at the heart of finding a job that suits you. Be sure to be specific about your answers.

1. What makes you happy at home?
2. What gives you satisfaction outside of work?
3. What's your best trait/skill? (If you're stuck, ask a friend.)
4. What's your worst trait/skill? (If you're stuck, ask a brave friend.)
5. What was the last thing that gave you a huge sense of achievement at work?
6. What's your dream job?
7. What's stopping you from getting that job?

Look at your answers and determine the two most important facts that come out about yourself. Are there hidden skills in your answers that you've never considered? Do your answers hint at a particular career?

EXAMPLE: JANE, 35. CURRENT JOB: SECRETARY IN A RECRUITMENT AGENCY.

1. What makes you happy at home?
Being in the outdoors, talking with friends and being creative.

2. What gives you satisfaction outside of work?
Making things, learning new things and feeling I get the most out of my spare time.

3. What's your best trait/skill?
I'm a good listener.

4. What's your worst trait/skill?
I get bored easily.

5. What was the last thing that gave you a huge sense of achievement at work?
Being asked to be part of a new team project.

6. What's your dream job?
I don't know.

7. What's stopping you from getting that job?
I have no skills.

Jane's answers point clearly to the fact that she is at her happiest when she is communicating with others and being creative with her time. The fact that she gets bored easily means that she needs a job that keeps her on her toes, and as she's a good listener, a job that makes her a team player would suit her best.

She says she has no skills but unwittingly she has the following hidden skills:

- **Secretarial skills**
- **Listening/people skills**
- **Creative skills**
- **Communication skills**
- **Time-management skills**

To find her ideal new job Jane should focus on what she means by 'creative' and think about a job that incorporates all of the above skills, such as public relations and marketing, and hone her skills accordingly.

STEP TWO:

Get rid of the 'I can't' mentality

The chances are that even if you've done the above exercise you're still thinking that your perfect job is out of your grasp. If so, it may help to know it's not you being negative but the ripple effect of being in a job that continually demoralises you.

Whether you're bored, under too much pressure, underpaid and unappreciated, or doing a job that doesn't suit you, it will eventually eat away at your confidence and self-esteem. So, if you've been doing a job unhappily for years, you need to ask yourself the following questions:

1. What makes you stay?

2. What positive rewards do you get from staying in this job?

Before you answer, be honest with yourself. Research shows we often keep doing something that makes us unhappy because it also gives us a positive feeling in some area of our life.

Possible answers to 'What makes you stay?':

- **The money.**
- **It's a job.**
- **I don't know what else I would do.**
- **I have bills to pay.**
- **I have kids to keep.**

Possible answers to 'What positive rewards do you get from staying in this job?':

- **I get lots of sympathy and attention from friends and family.**
- **I get paid well.**
- **I know I can do it with my eyes shut.**
- **They'll never fire me.**
- **They don't stop me from doing my own thing in their time.**

In order to break this pattern, you need to take yourself out of your comfort zone. Change is uncomfortable but not impossible, and if you plan it properly (see below) it won't leave you out of pocket and unemployed.

To help yourself do this you need to work out the roots of your work ethics. Start by asking yourself if you have strong memories of how your parents worked and talked about work. Did they toil away for all hours for little financial reward? Did they encourage you to get a job you liked, or hint that work was simply a means to an end? Did your parents have rewarding jobs, or jobs that crushed their spirits?

These messages are important because they lay the foundations of how you now think about work. Your attitude to a career will be either a replica of your parents or the direct opposite.

To help yourself, think about:

- **What positive and negative messages were you given about work and jobs when growing up?**

- When you told your parents what you wanted to be, was their response negative or positive?
- Did your parents live to work, or work to live?
- Did your parents have different attitudes to work?

Other possible messages you may have picked up are:

'Only fools work for a living' – Tina, 28

'What's the point of trying – you have to know someone to get on' – Maxine, 30

I'd be foolish to get above myself and try for a promotion' – Mary, 28

EXERCISE TWO

Does your work ethic reflect your mother's style, your father's style or neither?

1. List two beliefs you hold about women and work.

a. _____

b. _____

2. List two beliefs you hold about people who have their dream jobs.

a. _____

b. _____

The good news is, the beliefs that you hold about work and your abilities are thoughts that you can change, not facts written in stone. Just because you were told at home or school and/or by an ex-boss that you were, say, 'lazy', 'uncreative', or 'not made' for a certain career, doesn't mean that this is you. One way to change your beliefs about yourself is to challenge yourself actively to move out of your comfort zone each day. Start with small things such as standing up for yourself at work, and/or trying out something you've always been afraid of. Next, build your skill base. For example, it's no good whingeing that you can't be a teacher because you haven't got a maths qualification. If you want to be a teacher badly enough, join an evening class and get maths under your belt. To help yourself, list all the skills you think you're lacking and do something about it before the day is out.

Karen, 28, always wanted to work in Italy, but as a nursery nurse with no language skills, she used to complain that she couldn't speak Italian and so couldn't do it. At the age of 25 years she stopped complaining, enrolled in a weekly evening class, and a year later went off to work in Rome.

Jenny, 32, and her husband wanted to move out of the city and bring up their kids in the country, but as she was a human resources assistant for a TV company and he was a public relations man their jobs were specific to a life in the city. Their solution was to train to become web designers via an online course. A year down the line they moved to the country and set up an online design consultancy from their new home.

STEP THREE:

Give yourself a kick in the pants

In an ideal world you wouldn't wait for the worst to happen in order to do something about your job, but this is what often happens. A major life change, a redundancy, an office move or even an escalating intolerable situation pushes you to jump. The problem with this scenario is that it gives you no time to stop and think about what you want, as necessities such as paying bills often force you to take the next job that crosses your path. This is just one reason why it pays to stay alert in your working life. Every four weeks you should re-evaluate what's going on in your company and how you feel about your job, so that:

• **Nothing ever comes out of the blue and floors you.**

• **You can work on small problems before they become uncontrollably large ones.**

• **You can move jobs before you're pushed/let go/bored out of your mind.**

Envisaging the worst-case scenario (redundancy, the company going bankrupt) can also help you to find the motivation to change that you haven't been able to find so far. Help yourself by trying the following exercise:

EXERCISE THREE

Think about your life ten years from now.

1. How would you feel if you were still in the same job?

2. How would this affect your finances, your relationship and your health?

Think about your situation if you lost your job.

- How easy would it be for you to find a new one?

- What would stop you from finding a new job?

- What can you do (if anything) to safeguard yourself while in your present job?

The aim of this exercise is not to instil fear into you but to show you that you have to be proactive when it comes to changing jobs and careers. It's no good staying where you are and hoping that you'll get offered your dream job, or that you'll spot something spectacular in the paper one day. You have to get out there and look, invest in new skills, update your CV, ask around for new jobs, focus on what you want to do and, above all, get yourself moving.

TEN WAYS TO INVEST IN YOUR CAREER

1. Evaluate how your job is going every month.

2. Invest in new skills regularly.

3. Listen to constructive criticism.

4. Take measured risks with your job.

5. Aim high – don't wait until you are 'ready'.

6. Have long-term and short-term goals at all times.

7. Think about what makes you happy in normal life.

8. Think about what gives you job satisfaction.

9. Get the right support behind you.

10. Don't think only in terms of money when it comes to choosing a career.

CAREER REHAB
HOW TO MAKE THAT BREAK

Now that you recognise all is not perfect in your current job and you want to do better, it's time to look at how you can make changes and find out which direction might be the best for you. Looking at the different issues one step at a time will help you create your bigger picture.

1. Work out your career blocks

Career blocks are the excuses we give ourselves to avoid having to try. They may feel very real to us, but in 99.9 per cent of cases they can be overcome. Here's how:

I CAN'T AFFORD THE MONEY OR TIME TO RETRAIN

Finding a new job/career doesn't always take retraining, and if it does, building your skills can be done on a slower and more practical basis; for example, attending evening classes or an online/postal course. Many local colleges also offer support to people who can't afford fees, and if this isn't the case, look for loans that are specific to career development, as these come with a lower interest rate and deferred repayment. If time is an issue, bear in mind that the writer Stephen King wrote his first bestseller on the nightshift of his second job. Think about utilising your time in a different way – just an hour a day can make all the difference to skill building.

I'M TOO OLD TO START AGAIN

You don't have to start from scratch, simply start from where you are now. It's always difficult to change career completely, so if you feel you really can't do it all over again think about taking your present job into a new area. Jobs are rarely suited to only one type of company, and by adapting your skills and CV you could find yourself with a whole new lease of life, somewhere fresh and exciting.

I CAN'T COPE WITH THE PRESSURE OF CHANGING CAREERS

Worrying that you'll crumble under pressure is about the fear of failure. It is an instinctive reaction to a challenge and often happens when we're afraid to step out of our comfort zone. To help yourself, instead of trying to predict all the things that could go wrong (and have gone wrong in the past), break up the idea of a new career into manageable chunks that your brain can handle.

I'LL NEVER GET MY DREAM JOB, SO WHY BOTHER TRYING?

This is part of the I'm-not-worthy school of thought. Studies show that while men quite happily apply for the job of their dreams regardless of their skills, 90 per cent of women hold back, fearing they are not good enough.

The fact is, if you don't try you'll never know, and if you don't know you'll always wonder what you could have achieved. Don't be daunted by what seems like the impossible, if people are doing the job you want, there's no reason why you can't too.

I'M IN A RUT AND I CAN'T GET OUT

Being in a rut translates as being too afraid to move away from your comfort zone. It's always hard to move away from job security even if it makes you unhappy. However, it's only by challenging yourself that you can move forwards. Help yourself by getting a career buddy – someone who will push you to act on your complaints and look to new avenues.

I CAN'T GET A FOOT IN THE DOOR

After retraining to be a make-up artist, Sam, 34, spent 18 months sending endless copies of her CV to agencies hoping she'd get an appointment and a possible job. Fed up with their silence, she eventually cut out the middleman and wrote directly to TV production companies nailing an interview and getting a job on a soap opera. The moral is: if it's not working, change tactics.

2. Create your perfect job

To reboot a flagging career or find a new one, start thinking of your ideal job as a recipe.

THE INGREDIENTS

What elements/ingredients do you need for your new job to be perfect for you? For example:

- How many hours a day do you want to work?
- How much do you want to earn a year?
- Do you need/want job security?
- Do you need/want autonomy?
- Are you looking for glamour?
- Do you want/need credibility in your job?
- Do you want a job with kudos attached?
- Are you looking for rewards of a financial nature?
- Do you want to be part of a team?
- Do you want a career that's competitive?
- Do you want a low-stress job?

WHAT SKILLS DO YOU HAVE?

What elements/ingredients do you need for your new job to be perfect for you? For example:

Skills are abilities you are proficient in and can be anything from writing skills to listening skills to practical skills. If you feel you have zero skills, enlist the help of a friend and a family member to help you come up with at least five skills:

1. _____
2. _____
3. _____
4. _____
5. _____

WHAT SKILLS COULD YOU DO WITH?

We all know what areas we perform badly in, and what areas we need to boost. List three skills you could do with learning:

1. _____

2. _____

3. _____

Suzanne, 32, is a stay-at-home mum of three, who used to work in human resources for a magazine company but now wants a new career. She wants to:

- **Have flexible working hours and work from home.**
- **Be her own boss.**
- **Find a job that's creative.**
- **Make money.**

She lists her skills as:

1. **Good with people.**
2. **Proactive and practical.**
3. **Computer literate.**
4. **A good eye for design and detail.**
5. **Good at working on her own.**

She knows she needs to:

1. **Update her computer skills.**
2. **Get her English GSCE.**
3. **Boost her financial savvy.**

Therefore, potential new areas include website design, public relations, life coach, counsellor.

Be honest and practical about your answers. You may think being creative and/or not being told what to do are essential components for your ideal career BUT are you really creative? Can you easily come up with ideas and solutions? If you hate being told what to do, are you good at working on your own and using your own initiative? Expand your ideas about what may be right and wrong for you by expanding your answers about your skills and desires:

For example:
In what ways are you creative in your life?

_____

In what ways are you organised at home and at work?

_____

Are you better working on your own, or in a team? Give yourself an example from your work or social life.

_____

Is a 9.00 to 5.00 job important or would you prefer to work your own hours?

_____

Are you a team player? If so, give an example.

_____

If you like being in charge, are you good at motivating others? Give an example.

_____

What is it you hate about being told what to do by others?

_____

From your answers you should be able to get a clearer picture of what you're good at and what you want from a job. If no clear career leaps out at you, look at what you enjoy in your life. Hobbies and childhood pleasures are clues when it comes to what you want to do. The trick is to focus on what you enjoy, and then ask yourself why you enjoy it and then match this to your skills.

Hannah, 29, is a marketing assistant to a fashion chain but wants to change career. This is her list:

- **I love being outside, because I feel trapped in an office all day.**

  Key fact 1 Hannah needs a varied work environment.

- **I do voluntary work for a local animal shelter.**

  Key fact 2 Hannah feels strongly about animal causes.

- **I'm good when it comes to meeting new people.**

  Key fact 3 Hannah is a good communicator.

- **Secretly I feel my job is shallow.**

  Key fact 4 Hannah wants a more worthwhile career.

3. Use your initiative

Now put what you know about yourself (skills, attitude and what you want from your job recipe) into action. List all the careers you have a smattering of interest in. Not specific jobs, but specific areas that appeal to you, such as the media, the Internet, medicine, banking, teaching, or something else entirely. Don't think 'I'll never get into this' or 'I'm too old for this', just write down the area and be as open-minded as possible. The important thing to remember is that each job area contains hundreds of different jobs, some of which you don't even know about yet. Once you have your fields of interest:

BRAINSTORM IDEAS

Do this with a group of people who you respect, like and have something to offer; that is, they are positive. Remember: you don't have to go for a radical change to alter the direction of your career. Sometimes coming up with a small change, such as moving departments, changing your job within your company or changing the way you work, can make all the difference. Brainstorm all this and more to see what works for you and what doesn't.

RESEARCH YOUR FIELD OF INTEREST

Once you have a list of specific jobs within a field, go to the library and look these jobs up to see what they entail and what extra skills you may need. Also surf Internet job websites that list vacancies in your desired fields and read newspaper job adverts to see what companies are looking for. Pay special attention to jobs that recur frequently, as this gives you an idea of what's happening in the job market.

> **Good research options:**
> - **Business biographies**
> - **Newspapers**
> - **The Internet**
> - **People you work with**
> - **Friends**
> - **Family**
> - **Libraries**
> - **Television**
> - **Bookstores**

UTILISE YOUR CONTACTS
(BOTH PERSONAL AND PROFESSIONAL)

This means speak to anyone who works in the area you're interested in. Your aim is to find out as much about the field as possible, and what you need to do to get into this field. If you don't know anyone directly involved, ask friends of friends for help, and think about speaking (either in person or via email) with the people you used to work with or currently go to school or college with and asking for pointers. A good way to reach a large amount of people in a short space of time is to email everyone you know and ask them to pass on your request for information to anyone they know. It may sound desperate if you've never done it before, but this is what is known as networking.

4. Make it happen

By now you should be raring to go and find a new job or a new direction for your career. If so, it's time to set some goals. However, before you start, bear in mind that to make things happen your goals need to be realistic. Wanting to star in a soap opera when you've never acted, or write a book when you don't read, or even be a pop star when you can't sing or dance, tends to indicate that this is a dream, not a goal. Of course, you can make your dreams real, BUT only if you do something proactive about it. Meaning: stop talking and start doing.

Wherever you decide to head to, make a fully formed attempt to get the job you want. It's essential that you look back over your job recipe and your skills list and do the following:

GOAL NO. 1: ADAPT/LEARN AND UTILISE YOUR SKILLS

Ways to boost your skills include the obvious: evening classes and day-release college courses as well as the not so obvious finding a career mentor. This is someone you can observe and learn from. If you don't know anyone in the field of your choice, work experience or voluntary work within an organisation is always a good start. It also pays to know that although there are courses for all kinds of things, you can still get into a career without doing the prerequisite course or taking the normal route.

Just among my friends and acquaintances I know a secretary who became a bestselling author, a fashion stylist who used to work in a greengrocer's, a photographer who became an osteopath and a school dropout who became a consultant of cardiology at a top London hospital.

GOAL NO. 2: PRIORITISE YOUR CAREER GOALS (MAKE A LIST)

Aim high is the best advice. If you wait until you're ready for something you'll never go for it, so think big aims (long term) and small aims. Under big aims, dream up your future prospects. These are things you want to achieve in a year or longer, and they can range from the mundane (job security) to the sublime (a six-figure salary and your own office). Under small aims list the practical nitty-gritty stuff; that is, pay attention to details such as updating your CV, applying for jobs, getting on to relevant courses, fine-tuning your interview technique, and building a support group of people who can help.

CAREER FREEDOM
FINDING THE NEW YOU AND SELLING YOURSELF

Discovering what you're good at and finding ways to express that to a prospective employer is a maximum confidence booster. Improve your look and interview skills and you'll have the right combination to achieve your goal.

1. Brand yourself

Think you're bad at selling yourself? Rubbish at getting your message across and useless at showing prospective employers your true worth? Well, the good news is you can change all of the above; the bad news is you have to change it all. In an ideal world your amazing credentials and skills would immediately land you the job of your dreams. Unfortunately we live in a competitive workplace where there are plenty of people out there with the same skills at you. So, to get ahead of the field you need to work on your brand image.

This means start thinking of yourself as a brand that has something unique and exciting to offer. A way to do this is to consider a well-known brand (think of a sports one or a fizzy drink, or even a clothes brand) and ask yourself: within its competitive market, what puts this brand ahead of the rest?

The answer should be its USP – unique selling point – the statement that has you believing it's the best product out there, and therefore you should buy it. Of course, looking beneath the surface, USPs aren't so unique but they work because they tell people something they want to hear and this is what prospective employers want to hear from you.

To make yourself a brand you need to find your USP. My USP, when it came to selling features about relationships, lifestyle issues and health, was that I was an agony aunt with five years' worth of experience.

Kelly, 27, found that her USP when she became a personal trainer was that she used to be 25 kilos (55lb) overweight. This placed her ahead of the field when it came to securing new clients, because the new members at her gym knew she could relate to their problems. Hannah, 34, found her USP when she applied for a job as a primary school teacher was that she had a background in drama so could think on her feet and had no problem 'performing' in front of kids.

BUSINESS LETTERS

Part of branding yourself is knowing how to write a good business letter. This is your first port of call with a prospective employer and a good way to blow your chances of ever getting an interview. Speak to friends who recruit for their companies and you'll find that many candidates don't even get in the door because they don't bother to spell- or grammar-check their letter before sending it off. Others forget to enclose their contact details or even say what job they are applying for.

The number-one annoying thing you can do when applying for a job is wrongly spell the name of the person the letter is addressed to. It's guaranteed to annoy someone before they even get to your CV, and it suggests incompetence.

As an ex-commissioning editor of a teenage girls' magazine, I saw this first hand. Many people came for jobs with no idea what kind of magazine they were applying for or with ideas for features on subjects such as bell-ringing, tap-dancing and horses, when the magazine's emphasis was firmly on fashion and pop bands. Others claimed they 'hated teenagers', or cited 'getting to work on time' as a strength or 'stealing stationery' as their weakness. While you'll probably never say anything so foolish, it's an example of just how badly you can go wrong.

CLOTHING

A certain amount of conformity with your clothes also counts at job interviews. If you want to make an impact, then do it with your words and credentials not with your hair, make-up or clothes. The key to making a good first impression is to ensure that you look as if you already belong to the company; that is, smart, professional and clean. It sounds obvious but ask friends who recruit on a regular basis and you'll find that a good 50 per cent of interviewees don't bother to do any of those things.

BODY LANGUAGE

Studies show that we judge people not only on what they say but also on their body language, and tone of voice. So when you walk into a room and start talking, the message you send out to others registers in the following way:

55 per cent comes from your body language.

38 per cent comes from the tone of your voice, and your attitude.

7 per cent comes from what you actually say.

There is no secret code to body language, it's all fairly simple.

THINK POSTURE

Slumping or slouching into your seat, clenching your fists, biting your lip and looking at your feet screams 'weak and nervous'. Leaning forwards, gesticulating madly and moving your head a lot shouts 'confrontational'. To get your posture right, imagine a string pulling you up from the centre of your head. This should allow your shoulders to roll backwards and drop, and pull you upwards into good posture.

KEEP BREATHING

We all tend to hold our breath when we are nervous, and this in turn makes us feel sick and gives us that wobbly voice. So start by taking normal breaths. Then if you feel your voice breaking, breathe out, as this forces you to take an in-breath and restores your voice (breathe in first and the opposite will happen). If you want to firm up your voice when speaking, a good exercise is to read aloud to yourself or a friend. If you do this for five minutes every day it will help to calm your nerves in an interview.

MAKE THE RIGHT ENTRANCE

Most of us make up our minds about people within the first 20 seconds – so make sure your entrance counts. Bumbling into a room with shopping bags, newspapers and a coffee is not saying, 'I'm a professional person.' Striding in and grabbing someone's hand is also not appropriate. Judge each situation on its own merits. Walk in, make eye contact, smile and say hello. If a hand is offered, take it, if not, offer yours and sit down, and let the interview begin.

2. Preparation

If you really want the job you're going for, you owe it to yourself to prepare. You may have done all of the exercises above and researched your career inside and out but you also have to prepare for every interview you go for, and this means:

- **Understand the ins and outs of the job you're interviewing for.**
- **Know the background of the company.**
- **Know the strength of their USP (that is, what makes them special).**
- **Look up their profit margins and/or past successes and failures.**
- **Know what you could bring to the company.**

Knowing all of the above will help you to determine your interview strategy, which is the way you're going to persuade them that they should give you the job. Examples of ways to do this is to talk about a past success or failure they have had and how you would turn it around.

When getting a job at her local gym, Kelly, 27, pointed out in her interview that as an ex-member of another gym she had left because she felt the gym ignored their female clientele, and she came up with three ways they could have changed this. This was a clever tactic, since the gym she was approaching had a 90 per cent female clientele.

Also be prepared for sticky questions; they are the employer's way of separating the wheat from the chaff:

Question: You've changed careers a lot?/You've stayed in one place for a long time?

Make your answer positive. If you have a scattered CV, make it a plus by pointing out your expertise in various fields. If you've stayed in one place for a long time, push company loyalty and job satisfaction.

Question: Why do you want a new job?

Talk about challenges, and what you have to offer, but also be sure to talk about your present job and your boss in a positive way.

Question: What are your strengths and weaknesses?

Don't be humble or arrogant about your strengths, but at the same time don't list your flaws, or pretend you are perfect. Your prospective employer is looking to see that you have insight and self-awareness.

Question: What wage are you looking for?

Base your answer on the market rate plus a bit extra.

Question: Why do you want this job?

You'd think the answer would be obvious, but it's a question many candidates fall down on. Your answer should be no more than a sentence, and should involve you emphasising your USP.

Question: Tell me about yourself.

Not an invitation to get personal or relay your whole CV, but a chance to encapsulate your career to date briefly, say why you want a new job and slip in your USP.

3. Psychometric tests

It's also worth getting to grips with the tests you may be asked to take while at an interview. Many major companies now ask candidates to do some kind of psychometric testing, which are tests that assess your thinking. These include aptitude tests and personality tests that help to build up a profile of who you are. Aptitude tests aren't knowledge-based tests, but tests that deal with your reasoning and behaviour, whereas personality tests deal with your working style and the way you relate to others.

Get familiar with these tests, as some companies put a lot of stock in them. Check the Resources section for websites that give you an idea of what to expect. However, it's also worth remembering:

- **Test results are used only as part of the selection process, not in isolation. They are an additional source of information rather than the sole criterion on which a decision is made.**

- **Ask in advance if you have any questions about the tests. For example, let the company know if you have special needs (such as dyslexia).**

4. A word about prospective employers

Many employers are not good interviewers and you may come armed with a large amount of information that you want to get across but find you're never asked the right question. The way to get around this is to take the initiative and don't just answer yes and no, but find ways to add examples to your answers or spin questions around so that you can get vital information across. Be sure to maintain boundaries; that is, don't take over, don't be over-familiar and don't tell stories about your personal life. Try to keep the emphasis of your answers in a fine balance between what you have done in the past (transferable skills and successes) and what you would like to do in the future (what you can bring to the company).

Finally, come armed with the right questions. In the past I have heard interviewees say the following things when asked if they have any questions about the job: 'Would I be able to sit by a window?', 'What are the cafés like around here?', 'Is it OK to take days off when you have a hangover?' All big no-no's!

Ask questions that will tell you if this is the job for you; after all, an interview is also your chance to find out if the job fits. Questions to ask include those about the company culture, in-house training, and, finally, what the next step is after this interview.

One-month Career Makeover

The aim of the one-month planner is to take a step-by-step approach to sorting out your career. There are three basic rules:

1. **Do something for your career every day – even if it is just 20 minutes thinking time.**
2. **If you can't do the exercises then ask a friend for help and they can be your career buddy.**
3. **Don't listen to people who have nothing positive to add.**

'A personality clash with my new boss forced me to take voluntary redundancy from an event planning job and I just couldn't find another job. Two months into being unemployed a friend asked to help organise her wedding and I ended up doing all of it for her and loving it. An impressed guest asked me to arrange her 30th birthday party and from that I got another wedding. Suddenly I had a new career – Party Planning and I love it.'

KAREN, 26

WEEK ONE

MONDAY
Take an hour out and dream up your ideal job. Write it into a small notebook. The perfect job for you should contain skills you already have, skills you can get, and elements of life that you enjoy. Write down everything you want from this job.

TUESDAY
List everything you hate about your present job/career and include emotional as well as practical issues. Now work out what problems would be solved by changing jobs, and what problems would be solved by learning new skills.

WEDNESDAY
List your skills. If you have trouble identifying them, ask a friend to help you out. Work out which of these skills needs to be updated, and go online to find courses in your area.

THURSDAY
What brand-new skills will you need for your ideal job? If you don't know, research your job online and work out what you need to do to get from where you are now to where you want to be.

FRIDAY
If you are still unsure about what you want to do, spend the night brainstorming with friends and listen to their suggestions. Make a note of anything that sounds interesting and/or achievable.

SATURDAY
Scan the job vacancies in the Saturday papers and then go to the library and research any of the jobs that sound interesting.

SUNDAY
Think about how you're going to fund going on a course or changing careers. Think career-development loan, savings, and so on. Then make three decisions: (1) what job are you going to work towards? (2) what skills are you going to develop? and (3) how are you going to achieve (1) and (2)?

WEEK TWO

MONDAY

Sit down with friends and work out your strengths and weaknesses. To help yourself, have a go at some of the personality tests on online sites (see Resources). The aim here is to develop awareness about your skills.

TUESDAY

Seek professional advice (from recruitment agencies and career consultants) about your CV, or ask friends for advice on how they put theirs together.

WEDNESDAY

Spend a whole evening working on your CV. Show it to a friend and get feedback.

THURSDAY

Search for courses and new jobs in papers, online and with agencies. Make a note of anything you like the look of and draft an application letter to them.

FRIDAY

Today's the day to apply for a job or a course.

SATURDAY

Give yourself a weekend makeover. First, think of what impression you want to give to a prospective employer, and focus on grooming and an interview wardrobe.

SUNDAY

Invite friends over and role-play some interview scenarios.

WEEK THREE

MONDAY
Apply directly to three companies you'd like to work for, include your CV and tell them what you could offer the company.

TUESDAY
Consider joining a recruitment agency that specialises in what you want to do. Apart from giving you direct access to companies, they can also advise you on your CV.

WEDNESDAY
Start networking. Email/call friends and old work colleagues to see if they know of any jobs available or if they can offer any insight into an area you're trying to get into.

THURSDAY
Consider work experience on a voluntary basis or asking someone to be your career mentor; that is, offer you advice and information when you're stuck or lacking in motivation.

FRIDAY
If you can't find anyone who works in the career area you know, go to the business section of a bookstore or the library and hunt out biographies of business people – these books can offer a helpful insight.

SATURDAY
Think about a long-term career plan. This should incorporate where you want to be in five years, ten years and 20 years.

SUNDAY
If you're getting nowhere, look back over what you've done so far and list people you need to call tomorrow. There's no harm in calling companies to ask how the application process is going.

WEEK FOUR

MONDAY
Start preparing for an interview. What's your USP (Unique Selling Point)?

TUESDAY
Research the companies you have applied to so that you have background information at hand.

WEDNESDAY
Think about how you're going to talk about your job weaknesses – how can you spin these into a positive? Then think about questions you can ask at the interview.

THURSDAY
Don't put all your eggs in one basket; keep looking for new jobs and courses to add to your skills.

FRIDAY
If you haven't got an interview yet, go back and work out alternate ways you can get into this career. Could you do freelance work, contract work or approach the company in a different way?

SATURDAY
Work out who your career support team is – these should be the people who have been supporting and encouraging you. Get together with them and brainstorm new ideas.

SUNDAY
Consider your unfulfilled skills; that is, what you'd like to be able to do but so far haven't gone for – and simply go for it!

Finance

Introduction

Money, money, money – whether it makes your world go round or grind to a halt, the facts are simple: we could all do with a bit of help when it comes to how we deal with our cash. You may think: why bother, after all it will work out in the end, but the fact is unless you make a decision to take control of your finances today, nothing is likely to work out tomorrow. Meaning, no wonderful house to live in one day, no fancy holidays abroad and no savings to see you through weddings, births and even your old age.

So, if you're someone who is afraid to open your bank and credit card statements, worried every time you use an ATM machine, and unsure of how much you owe – you need this section, and you need it fast. Don't fool yourself – just because you get by on a wing and a prayer now, sooner or later your debt will catch up with you. Sooner or later you will have to pay back what you owe, so why not take control of it and do it now? If not for the sake of your future, then definitely for the sake of your sanity.

And that, in a nutshell, is the real problem with debt: it's always there lurking at the back of your mind, ready to weigh down on you like a ton of bricks and make you depressed and scared. The fact is no one is ever happily in debt, even if they ring up credit charges every day. Debt not only crushes your chances of a happy and secure present but also a happy and secure future.

Now for the good news: even if you're befuddled by the thought of money management, feel upset when you read a financial document and/or are generally appalled by the shape of your financial health, you can do something about it, and fast. You don't even have to be an expert or a financial whiz to get your head around figures and repayments. Financial management may be dull but it's not difficult, and even the biggest debts have a solution as long as you're prepared to change your spending behaviour and put in time and effort.

This tactic usually entails a three-pronged approach: (1) make a decision to change your habits; (2) be honest with yourself; and (3) face your debts head-on. Do all of these and you're halfway to changing your financial future. So, whether it's despair or the realisation that you're heading for financial meltdown that's brought you to this section, here's how to uncover the new financial you.

Quiz

WHAT'S YOUR FINANCIAL STYLE?

Self-awareness is key when it comes to making changes of any type. No matter how well you think you know yourself and how you ended up where you are, the chances are you're missing the bigger picture. The following quiz and exercises are designed to give you a clearer insight into your attitude to money and spending. Go with your gut feeling when answering, then look at the next page for the results.

1. **You've had a terrible day at work and want to make yourself feel better. Do you:**
   a. Treat yourself to a bar of chocolate/a drink? **(B)**
   b. Go for a blow-out meal at a fancy restaurant or make an expensive purchase? **(BS)**
   c. Go home to bed? **(W)**
   d. Have a night in with a bottle of wine, a DVD, a takeaway and new set of beauty products? **(OS)**

2. **The last time you maxed-out on your credit card and went overdrawn, it was because:**
   a. You had x number of birthdays, a wedding and then some unexpected bills came in, and you just had to buy x. **(OS)**
   b. You treated yourself to a holiday/expensive purchase. **(BS)**
   c. You have been overspending for the last year. **(B)**
   d. You have never been overdrawn because you never go to the limit of your finances. **(W)**

3. **Do you know how much money is in your current account and how much you owe right now?**

a. Approximately. **(BS)**
b. To the last cent/penny. **(W)**
c. No, but you know when you get paid. **(OS)**
d. Yes, but you do not how much you owe. **(B)**

4. **It's the week before payday, and you need money. Do you:**
    a. Withdraw cash on your credit cards. **(BS)**
    b. Go over your agreed overdraft level. **(OS)**
    c. Feel like it's the end of the world. **(W)**
    d. Borrow from friends and family. **(B)**

5. **Do you have a nest egg for the future?**
    a. No, but you're relying on a future inheritance to get by. **(OS)**
    b. Yes – your property. **(BS)**
    c. No, and you're sick when you think about it. **(W)**
    d. A small amount you never ever touch. **(B)**

6. **How do you make yourself feel better about your debts?**
    a. You tell yourself it's a normal part of modern life. **(BS)**
    b. You reassure yourself that you're not as in debt as some people. **(OS)**
    c. You don't! **(W)**
    d. By looking at your savings even if they're smaller than your debt. **(B)**

7. **How do you hope to pay off your debts?**
    a. By winning the lottery. **(BS)**
    b. By getting a lucky windfall. **(OS)**
    c. By marrying someone better off than you are. **(B)**
    d. With a strict budget. **(W)**

8. **Which best sums up your attitude to your finances?**
    a. It stresses you out to the point of tears. **(OS)**
    b. Life's too short to worry about money. **(BS)**
    c. You hope for the best. **(B)**
    d. You worry about it constantly. **(W)**

Results

Add up all the answers you gave that were followed by **(BS)** and then those followed by **(OS)**, and so on. Then see which score was the highest. If you scored highest on the **(BS)** answers that makes you a Big Spender, see below. If you scored highest on the **(OS)** answers that makes you an Over-spender, and so on.

BIG SPENDER (BS)

You like to spend money and your thrill comes from the sheer joy of buying big. The chances are you're not only in debt but you've also given up thinking about paying back what you owe. Your view is: live today, pay one day in the distant future! Your bravado is all well and good but have you considered just how you're going to pay back your debt? The problem with credit is that one day it stops, and when that happens it's payback time. Don't give yourself the hope that something will just turn up, because the people who turn up will be the bailiffs, and your creditors. Face facts: it's time to pay today for what you lived on yesterday.

OVER-SPENDER (OS)

Shopaholic ahoy! You have a treat mentality and it's getting you into big trouble. Whether you're trying to buy yourself a lifestyle or shopping to make yourself feel better only you can say, but one thing's for sure: you can't afford your extravagant lifestyle, and somewhere deep inside you know it.

Your real problem is you can't, or won't, face reality. Meaning, it's time to cut up your credit cards, open all your bank statements, and total up all that you've spent. Far from it being depressing, you'll be amazed at how empowered you feel by taking control. Still unsure? Well, the next time you see a must-have purchase, weigh up the thrill of the buy against all those sleepless nights you currently have worrying about how you're going to get by.

BALANCED-UP (B)

When it comes to finances you live in the present, working from day to day with what you have. You may not have any money left come pay day but you know next month's wages will take care of that. You happily repay your minimum payments and even have a small blow-out now and again. Maybe you even have a small amount of savings, but the question is: what about the future? Prince Charming isn't going to waltz in and whisk you off to financial happiness. You need to plan, save and invest in order to ensure you have money for the future. Time to take a look at the bigger picture.

WORRIER (W)

You're scared of money, financial planning and even getting into debt. Maybe financial documents confuse you, or you don't think you have the right mind for money. Perhaps, you were brought up with a doom-and-gloom attitude to investments and savings, and a strict idea that all debt is bad. You need to realise that money management isn't difficult. It's just a fact of life and one that anyone is capable of handling. Don't be afraid of what you don't know. Educate yourself – you won't be sorry.

FINANCIAL THERAPY

FACING THE FACTS ABOUT YOURSELF

If you fall into the 'useless with money' category, the good news is you don't need a slap on the wrist or intensive therapy to 'get better' but you do need to learn how to manage the cash that flows through your fingers. It sounds obvious, but I know from experience that common sense isn't so common when you can't see the wood for the trees. The trouble is, unless you were blessed with parents with financial savvy, the chances are you, like most people out there, have never been taught how to be good with money.

In your head you probably know what you 'should' be doing; that is, not overspending and living beyond your means, but if you're already in debt or have no idea how to make your money go further without overspending, it can be a struggle to get to grips with life's expenses. Which is why real financial change, like any kind of life change, is a tough nut to crack. It not only takes effort to challenge old financial beliefs but also a certain amount of will not to slip back into old habits when the going gets tough. However, it's worth knowing that people change their financial 'luck' every day, not with a windfall or a lottery win but by learning how (1) not to be afraid of money; and (2) how to make their money work for them.

If you've never balanced a chequebook in your life this probably sounds unlikely and overwhelming, but keep telling yourself that money management is not rocket science.

If you can add and subtract and/or use a calculator, you can manage your money. If you're good at juggling your money around to pay off one loan against another, and/or manage to eat and still find some money to buy that must-have item, you can save and build yourself a very healthy financial portfolio. As for being too lazy to think about your money issues, it's worth knowing that apathy will not only cost you thousands over a lifetime but also limit your future choices (where is the money going to come from to get married in style, bring up children or retire happily?).

STEP ONE:

WARNING – financial doom ahead!

Are you in a financial mess? Can you hold up your hand and say, 'I'm in big trouble – help me'? Does the thought of making such a statement make you nervous, queasy and/or sick to the stomach? If so, you're not alone. When I was in debt up to my ears, the very last thing I would ever have told anyone was that I needed help to sort out the mess I had got myself into. Although I was happy to throw my hands up and laughingly admit I was rubbish with money, I would never admit that I had huge debts because I had frittered away thousands and had nothing to show for it.

The reason for this was simple: I knew that admitting I was in trouble meant admitting I had to do something about it, and fast. So, if, like me, you're currently someone who is sick of being penniless by the end of the month, terrified of letters from your bank and have a stick-your-head-in-the-sand policy when it comes to paying back what you owe, it's time to hold up your hand and look at the reality of your situation.

Clues that you're heading for financial doom are:
- **Telling yourself you can always declare yourself bankrupt.**
- **Hoping you'll win the lottery or marry someone rich.**
- **Constantly telling yourself that some people are worse off than you.**
- **Having no savings or long-term financial plans.**
- **Having more than one credit card and store card, a loan and an overdraft.**

- **Never paying any more than the minimum payment on your cards.**
- **Not being sure of exactly how much you owe and to whom.**
- **Having no idea how much is currently in your bank account.**
- **Living a lifestyle your income can't support (that is, spending more than you earn).**
- **Spending more on going out, clothes and holidays than you do on rent/mortgage, bills and savings.**

It's scary stuff to take in, but speak to anyone who has got out of debt and you'll see that admitting there is a problem is the first step to financial freedom. To help unravel the financial lies from the financial truth, try the following exercise.

EXERCISE ONE

List three things you tell yourself to make yourself feel better about your financial situation.

_____   _____   _____

Now ask yourself:

1. How realistic are these statements? For example, is the equity in your property really equal to that of your debt? Will a windfall really drop from the sky and sort you out? Do your savings outweigh your debts?
2. What would really happen to you if you stripped away these 'reassuring' thoughts? Would the situation actually be any worse than it is?
3. What would it take to make you face your financial problems? A letter from bailiffs? A court date? Are you willing to let it go this far?

STEP TWO:

Get rid of the 'I deserve' mentality

It doesn't take a financial genius to work out that most people are usually in debt because they have hugely overspent in some way, or had to pay out a large amount of money for something such as a university degree. So, in order to untangle your finances and work on reducing your debt, you have to work out a budget that shows you what your money is going on, and why.

In an ideal world, if you work hard and pay your taxes you deserve a good living. However, what constitutes a good living in your head has to correspond to your income or else you're in big trouble. Going on five-star holidays, buying designer labels and dining out every night on credit rather than cash means you can't afford the life you lead no matter how much you think you deserve it. This is a painful concept to get around and even harder to beat if you love the life you lead and feel that it says a lot about who you are. If this is your current thinking, you need to look at your sense of entitlement and decipher what it's based on.

What will help is knowing how and why you got to where you are right now. Whereas overspending and living beyond your means are the roads to debt, discovering why you got on this path in the first place is the place where change begins. For most of us this means working out the roots of our financial behaviour by looking back to our childhoods.

Do you have strong memories of how your parents managed money and/or advised you how to manage it? Maybe you remember your parents fighting about cash, or saw your father take control of the household budget. Or perhaps your parents lived a lavish lifestyle of live-today-and-pay-tomorrow, or told you that it didn't matter how hard you tried because only the rich get rich.

These messages are important because they lay the foundations of how you now think about money. Your attitude to finances today will be either a replica of your parents' or a rebellion against their attitude.

To help yourself look at the past, ask yourself:

1. **What positive and negative messages were you given about money when growing up?**

2. **When you wanted money for something, how did your parents respond to your request?**

3. **Were your parents frugal or big spenders?**

4. **Did your parents have different spending styles?**

In looking at how your parents spent and saved, try to highlight clear messages you picked up about how to manage or not manage your money. For example, are you like Tina, 33, who is hugely in debt after learning from her mother that 'You shouldn't let lack of money stop you from having the life you want'? Or Alison, 28, whose father was so frugal that when she left home she went the other way and racked up a debt that was more than her yearly take-home salary.

Other possible messages you may have picked up are:

'Don't spend what you don't have' – Sal, 26

'Everyone's in debt – it's not a problem' – Dawn, 30

'Treat yourself – you deserve it' – Jane, 32

'Save, save, save' – Emma, 28

'Men should take care of the money' – Claire, 28

'Women are frivolous with cash' – Tina, 33

Knowing what your past financial lessons were is a huge step towards changing your beliefs about your ability to manage money in the present. Try the following exercise to highlight your spending habits.

EXERCISE TWO

1. Does your spending style reflect your mother's style, your father's style or neither?

2. List two beliefs you hold about women and money.

   a. _____

   b. _____

3. List two beliefs you hold about rich people.

   a. _____

   b. _____

Remember, no matter what you've listed, beliefs are not written in stone, which means you can change the ones you've listed above at any time by proving to yourself that they are wrong. One way to do this is to read up on finances and biographies of self-made millionaires. In doing so you'll see that rich people aren't always born rich and that turning your finances from poorly to healthy is not down to luck, but planning.

As for changing the beliefs you hold about yourself and money, you need to start telling yourself you can cope with money and be good at it. Remember: what we tell ourselves about our abilities and skills have major repercussions in our lives. Keep maintaining that you don't know what to do with money and you can't manage your finances and you'll make these things a self-fulfilling prophecy.

STEP THREE:

Give yourself a kick in the pants

Nobody has ever changed without a big kick in the pants. Sometimes this kick will come from an outside source (the bank, a credit company, or a threat of legal action) and sometimes from the people who love us (a partner or your family), or sometimes from a sense that you have to do something now or you never will. If you're looking for motivation to change and you haven't yet been convinced by the above information, here's a sure way to get your financial skates on.

The aim of this exercise is not to frighten you into a deep, dark gloom but to get you to see that what you owe today has serious consequences on how you live tomorrow. You may not want to live like a king, but by overspending now you are seriously limiting your choices for the future and putting things like buying a flat or even getting married the way you want to out of reach. So, every time you feel your willpower flagging, imagine the worst-case scenario overleaf (e.g. no. 6) and you'll instantly find your motivation to change.

EXERCISE THREE

1. Write down three things you would ideally like to have in ten years' time. They could include a house, a flash car, and two children, even a mountain of designer clothes.

   a. _____

   b. _____

   c. _____

2. Now calculate how much you owe. That's everything from outstanding loans owed to friends and family, overdrafts, loans on cars, loans from the bank, hire-purchase payments (no matter if it's 0 per cent interest), credit card debts, store card debts (the whole amount, not just minimum monthly payments), unpaid bills, both outstanding and new.

3. Now calculate how much you earn in a year. Write down your annual wage, any money that might come your way for bonuses in a year, birthday money and interest on savings, and your savings.

   _____

   _____

   _____

4. Compare what you owe against what you earn, and then see how likely those dreams seem now.

5. If this doesn't give you a big enough fright, deduct all your monthly outgoings from what you earn (rent, social life, travel, bills, insurance, and so on). and now compare that figure to what you owe.

6. Finally, no matter how unlikely it seems, imagine if you lost your job tomorrow. How would you survive now?

STEP FOUR:

Start a spending diary

There's no way around it, if you want to sort out your finances you have to know what's happening to them every minute of the day, not just when your monthly statements arrive. Accounting for your money isn't about fancy computing sheets, employing an accountant and even spending hours each day looking over your expenditure. A simple way to keep check of your cash flow is to keep a spending diary that accounts for every bit of money that goes in and out of your bank account on a daily basis.

The way to do this is simple. Carry a small notebook, keep all your receipts and start by writing in today's date and your current balance. Don't just guess at this figure; call up your bank and get an accurate figure. If you start with the wrong figure your cash flow will be wrong all month.

Now, as you go through the day, write down everything you spend and what the money was for. This includes cash taken from an ATM, debit payments in shops, direct debits out of your account, bill payments, and standing orders. In your diary notebook, note what you're spending your cash on, whether it's a bus ticket and newspaper, a pair of shoes or a pint of milk.

EXERCISE FOUR

1. After a week, look over your diary notebook and search for patterns in your spending. For example, what day did you 'treat' yourself to, and why? Do you spend more when you're unhappy or happy? Do you often buy more than one book at a time, or buy fast food because you can't be bothered to cook? Where does your money go and why?

2. What purchases in your week do you now regret or have already forgotten about, and how much is the total cost of these products?

3. Which social events cost more than you accounted for in your head?

4. Are there any bills/payouts/expenditure that came out of the blue or you forgot about and have left you in debt?

Knowing why and how you spend is an important part of sorting out your finances. If you know your weak money spots, you can do something about them. However, if you walk around in what's known as a waking sleep, you will let your cash trickle away bit by bit until you literally have nothing left.

Be alert to what you're doing with your cash and what people are charging you for their services (more of this later) because there are plenty of ways you can save money by just waking up to what you're doing.

'I wish I'd never got into debt and could have foreseen the misery it would bring me. From a teenager I was always spending my pocket money and hard-earned cash from my part-time job on clothes, shoes and going out. It was all part of self-esteem issues that I had, where I thought buying that pair of jeans, having my hair done or being 'seen' up the pub would in some way make me more accepted or popular . . .

Then I got into the cycle of trying to live at the pace that everyone else did, while coping with debts that most of them didn't have – why shouldn't I go on that holiday, or that night out? However, it just meant that when I did, my debts only got bigger. So now even though I'm earning a good wage, I'm struggling and doing two jobs to keep myself solvent and able to keep my lifestyle going.

My advice is to not fall into the trap of thinking that credit cards and loans are your own money! As my bank manager once said to me . . . "Your cheques don't go to some bank in the sky – they come here!"'

ANNA, 38

FINANCIAL REHAB
DEALING WITH YOUR DEBT

Hopefully, you're now fired up with resolve on how to fix your
finances, but before you do something radical it's worth bearing
in mind that it doesn't pay to be too zealous about your financial
goals. Attacking your life with zest is one thing, but being frugal
to the point of stinginess leads to burn-out, unless you are
embedded with heaps of willpower (which I am guessing you're
not). The key to lasting financial change is to start with small
steps that work towards the larger goal of financial freedom.
Here's how:

1. Know your monthly, weekly and daily budget

Yes, budget, as in draw up a budget, stick to a budget and have a
budget! If the word strikes the fear of God into your heart it's likely
you have no idea how much money goes in and out of your account
each month, never mind each day. A budget is the starting point for
the new financial you, so here's what to write down:

YOUR BUDGET

Income per month ————————————————

Outgoings per month ————————————————

OUTGOINGS – ESSENTIALS

Mortgage/rent per month
_____

Gas
_____

Electricity
_____

Telephone
_____

Water
_____

Service charge
_____

Insurance
_____

Council/state tax
_____

Travel costs
_____

Credit card/store payments
_____

Loan payments
_____

Other money owed
_____

Food
_____

Home supplies
_____

TOTAL:

The money that's left is now your budget for the month. Divide it by four to find your weekly budget. All your non-essentials need to be paid for out of this amount. If there's not much money left, this is the area to make cutbacks in.

OUTGOINGS – NON-ESSENTIALS

Meals out (including lunch and coffees)

Drinks (alcoholic)

Mobile phone/Internet

Books/magazines/newspapers

Cinema/DVDs/videos/CDs

Gym membership

Presents

Clothes

Beauty (including hair)

Miscellaneous

TOTAL:

Can you go out less? Eat in less expensive places? Take lunch to work? Not buy any more clothes and CDs? Go to the library instead of buying books? Cut out the gym membership and generally change your lifestyle? You may be screaming 'NO WAY!' but the reality is if you want financial freedom, you need to cut your costs in half (1) so that you are left in credit not overdraft by the month's end; and (2) so that you can pay back your debts at a faster rate.

For example, could you cut the following?

- **Have breakfast at home instead of buying a newspaper, coffee and a muffin on the way to work.**

- **Make lunch and bring a book instead of buying a sandwich and a magazine every day.**

- **Bring in snacks to the office instead of buying them.**

- **Make a meal and watch TV.**

Work out how much this would save you in a week and a month.
Total spend for 1 day = _____
Total spend for 1 week = 1 day x 5 = _____
Total spend for month = 1 week x 4 = _____

You don't have to be this radical to see savings. Just replacing your coffee-and-muffin habit each day can save a lot each month. You may think that small changes mean nothing when you owe thousands, but bear in mind that saving a bit each day will add up to a lot over a year.

If saving drastically from your non-essentials is not enough to make a huge dent in your debt, then take a long, hard look at your essential list. Are you living somewhere that's too expensive for your budget? Are you running a car when you don't need to? Are you paying high interest on credit cards, store cards and loans? These are areas you need to pay attention to, as you can save money here and cut back.

CREDIT CARDS

Do you have more than one card? If so, why? Do you have a 0 per cent interest deal? If not, what interest are you being charged, and for how long? What costs are there when you take money out on your credit card (the interest is higher for credit cards than that charged for a bank loan)? Are there any penalties for late payments or fees for services?

GET RID OF YOUR STORE CARDS

The interest and penalty fees are huge on store cards and they should be avoided at all costs. Cut the cards up and concentrate on paying them back.

WHAT'S YOUR MOBILE PHONE TARIFF AND INTERNET CONNECTION FEE?

Call up your service provider and ask – and don't trust them when they say this is the best deal for you. Work it out for yourself. Do you really need to chat for ages on your mobile phone at a premium rate when you can call from home at a cheaper rate or, better still, send an email or text? Is your Internet provider giving you a rate that suits your needs?

WHAT ARE YOUR CAR, MOBILE PHONE AND HOME INSURANCE PREMIUMS?

Do you know how much you're paying a year? Is it competitive? Check out the web for companies that offer savings, and check your statements to see what you're being charged each month.

TEN WAYS TO SAVE APPROXIMATELY 10 PER CENT OF YOUR WAGES A MONTH

1. Don't go out during the week – only at the weekend.

2. Cook home-made meals at home every weekday evening.

3. Eat breakfast at home.

4. Take lunch into work.

5. Don't rent DVDs.

6. Cancel your gym membership, if you don't go more than once a week.

7. Use your mobile phone only for emergencies.

8. Before you buy anything, ask yourself: do I really need this?

9. Swap magazines and books with friends.

10. Pay using cash – leave your credit and debit cards at home when you go out.

2. Don't ignore your creditors

Ignoring your bank manager and those nasty letters that come through the post from credit companies won't make your debt go away (or your creditors). What's more, as banks and credit companies like to make money from your overspending, borrowing excessively from 'helpful' creditors is also a way to avoid facing your debt.

Firstly, it's important to note that credit companies/banks/loan companies get aggressive only when they think you're ignoring them. So, open those letters and tell them you're having problems. If your creditors are aggressive and/or charging you huge fees, contact one of the debt agencies (see Resources).

Now ask yourself: do you have a plan when it comes to paying back what you owe, or are you just hopeful that one day you'll get to the end of your credit debt? Having a real end in sight is essential, for three reasons:

1. **It will help you to feel in control of your finances and future.**
2. **It will motivate you to focus on your efforts.**
3. **It will stop you feeling depressed and hopeless.**

More importantly, it will get you out of debt. It may take five years, but the sooner you start working on it, the sooner your debt-free point will come along. The starting point for financial rehab is, therefore, to work out how big your debt is.

WHAT YOU OWE

Credit cards

Store cards

Bank/store/credit company loans

Personal loans from friends and family

Overdrafts

Hire-purchase items

Miscellaneous debts

TOTAL:

Does the total amount (1) shock you; (2) make you want to cry; or (3) amount to approximately the amount you knew? Answers 1 and 2 are the usual ones here, simply because most of us rarely take the time to weigh up the greater picture for fear of actually knowing. And, let's face it, if your debt outweighs your income the greater picture is that your future choices are somewhat limited.

If your debts are large it could well take years to pay them off, and, as tempting as it is to use this as an excuse to not do anything, bear in mind that the longer you ignore your debt the longer it will take to be debt-free.

3. Create a repayment plan that prioritises your debts

To get out of debt, the good news is that you don't have to win the lottery but you do need to create a repayment plan that's based on figures that work for you; sadly, this means a repayment plan that's going to sting and mean cutbacks everywhere. There's no getting away from it, financial rehab hurts, but the pain is there for good reasons: (1) it stops you from doing it again; and (2) it makes you focus on the job at hand.

If you're switching off at this point and feeling that I don't understand the particular circumstances you are facing and/or that everyone has debts these days, it's time to remind yourself of the feelings you have about your debt, the added stress it puts on your life and the way it limits your choices.

However, having said that you should expect your repayment plan to hurt, there's no point in trying to pay back £200/$200 a month if it leaves you with only £10/$10 a week to survive on. Not only will you be doomed from the start if your repayment plan is too harsh but also your plan will last about two weeks.

For an effective repayment plan you need to:

- **Look at what you've put aside in your budget to pay off your debts and find a larger figure that makes you wince. Remember, the bigger your payback the faster you'll reach your goal. It's a bit like going on a diet: if you cut back on all the chocolate you eat you'll get thinner faster than the person who cuts back to just one bar a day.**

- **Next, bear in mind that paying back minimum payments means you'll never pay back what you owe, so budget for larger repayments (see the list of debts below).**

- **Start by prioritising your debt. Write a list of all your debts (look on your statements), starting with the loan/credit card that has the highest interest rate rather than the highest amount borrowed.**

Your aim should be to pay the highest amount back to the card/loan with the highest interest rate because this is your largest money pit. If all your cards hold the same interest, pay off the biggest loan first. This way you whittle that debt down as quickly as possible.

Be sure always to pay on time, because all banks and credit companies have fees for late payment (and even a day counts).

LIST OF ALL DEBTS

Creditors	Per cent interest	Amount owed	Monthly payback amount	Debt-free date
Store card 1				
Store card 2				
Credit card 1				
Credit card 2				
Loan				
Overdraft				

WARNING!

Along the way, as your debt decreases the company you have borrowed from is likely to start getting friendlier and offering you bigger incentives to spend with them. Incentives such as loyalty points, cashback promises and/or a bigger balance or new card because you're such a 'good' customer. Stay firm; the idea is to pay back what you owe, not owe more and as soon as you've paid off a card cancel the account (you should already have cut the card up).

If your debt is huge and the above plan seems pointless, it's time to think about borrowing a lump sum to pay off your debt and then paying back just that lump sum. This can be done with a consolidated bank loan. Even though you may end up paying more interest, this route works as long as you aren't tempted to spend and borrow more along the way just because in your head you start believing that one payment amount means you're debt-free. Remember your debt remains the same, whether it's spread over five accounts or rolled into one lump sum.

4. Be realistic about your savings and assets

Are you someone who owes £15,000/$15,000 but feels safe because you have savings of £5,000/$5,000?

Well, I hate to point this out, but you don't have savings, because in reality you owe £10,000/$10,000 and that's without the growing percentage interest on your debts. Therefore, it's foolish to have savings when your debts are growing steadily each month.

While it's essential to have a safety net for two months' rent, or mortgage (to get this, save 10 per cent of your income starting now, see below), excess savings above this amount, when you owe thousands, is a waste of time. Drop the debt first because this is what is going to help you in the future, not your savings, which means it's time to take a long, hard look at your assets. Assets are the investments that make you money after you've bought them (if you don't have any, don't despair, there's still time to get some, see Financial, Freedom below).

Now work out what your assets are:

WHAT ARE YOUR ASSETS?

ASSET	WORTH
Property (current market value)	
Savings	
Tax-free savings	
Shares	
Pension	
Miscellaneous (incl. jewellery)	

It's worth remembering that, although property is an asset, the worth of your house is in its equity – that's the money you've made on the purchase, after paying off your mortgage.

5. Learn to live sensibly

Also known as: find a lifestyle, don't try to buy one, which means learn to spot your spending triggers and squash them before they take control. This is not only the secret to happiness but it will also stop you waking up at 3.00 a.m. worrying about the state of your financial future.

One way to do this is to consider some retail therapy. Most of us get into debt by buying what we want, rather than what we need and what we can afford. Take Justine, 35; she earns £28,000/$28,000 a year, owes around £4,000/$4,000 on credit cards, and has an overdraft she regularly goes over. Yet, far from tightening in her financial belt, Justine drives a top-of-the-range car, has monthly pedicures, massages and facials, holidays at five-star hotels across the world and wears designer clothes, all bought on more credit.

You might say, 'Why shouldn't I have what I want now? I don't want to be sixty to have to wait for a sports car or designer watches. I want to live life now, and the future will take care of itself.'

'It's not fair', is the cry of most people who want a life they can't afford. If you want more, you have a number of choices:

UP YOUR EARNINGS

Either find a second job or find a new job; alternatively, train for a new career that has a higher income bracket. Upping your earnings is also the best way to decrease your debt at a speedier rate. Think of an evening bar job, being a waitress, reception work in a gym, or even joining a babysitting agency.

CUT BACK IN LESS IMPORTANT AREAS

If you want fancy holidays abroad, cut the amount of money you spend on clothes and socialising in your daily life. Or get rid of your car, and downsize your life.

GET RID OF YOUR DEBT

Yes, sorry, back to that old chestnut. Nothing will lead you to the life you want faster than offloading your debts and being debt-free. Paying back all you owe mean down the line you will be able to:

- **Have money for treats.**

- **Have money to put down a deposit on a house.**

- **Have money to get married.**

- **Have money to bring up a child.**

- **Have money to splash out and then really enjoy what you've bought.**

- **Have money to be generous and feel good about it.**

- **Have money to save for your future.**

- **Feel secure about your future.**

- **Feel less stressed about the 'what ifs'.**

- **Feel you can make plans because you know that you can afford it.**

6. A word about financial coupledom

Love conquers all – well it won't if money is a subject you can't discuss with your partner without war breaking out. So ask yourself: are you on the same financial wavelength – happy to save, spend and plan the same things? If so, you're in the minority. Studies show that money is the number-one source of conflict between couples, and it's hardly surprising because unless you have had identical upbringings, you're dealing with two sets of values and two sets of beliefs about how to handle cash.

Janine, 35, says she and her husband fall out constantly over money:

'The problem is we have totally different spending styles, I save and pay my bills when they come in, while he is a "live today, pay tomorrow" kind of guy. He believes he shouldn't have to change the way he lives, but his spending impacts on my life – we can't afford to move to a larger house, and I can't afford to be a stay-at-home mum, simply because his debts are overwhelming, so I'm left supporting our household on my wage.'

Hannah, 32, has the opposite problem and finds herself telling lies to her husband in an attempt not to inflame the already sensitive subject of her large debt:

‘I hide all my new clothes in my wardrobe or under the bed, and when Stephen asks me, "Is that new?" I always pretend it's an old thing he's seen before. I think he knows I'm lying but doesn't want to get into a fight, so we play this make-believe game until the bills come in, and then he goes ballistic. It's a ritual we go through every month.’

Love and money don't often go hand in hand, especially if one of you is a spendthrift and the other is a saver, or if one of you earns considerably more than the other. A discussion about finances can often lead to defensiveness, anger and stubbornness about what's mine is mine, and what's yours is yours. However, if you intend to build a future together, sooner or later you need to tackle your financial future. To help yourselves:

1. Agree that your financial future is a joint venture you will both take equal responsibility for. If you think it's a man's responsibility, think again, because whether you like it or not, gone are the days when the financial burden was all left to one person.

2. Discuss the attitudes and advice about money that you both grew up with, and see if you can find common ground to build your family's financial growth on.

3. Don't assume that one of you is right and one is wrong, your aim should be to find a middle financial ground somewhere between what both of you believe.

4. Agree that your debts are going to limit your future choices and make a pay-off plan that gets you to a debt-free point.

5. Don't pool all your money just because you're a couple. Think about a joint saving fund and joint household account, but also be accountable for your own money and debt.

6. Divide the monetary responsibility – don't take control of finances just because you're better with money, or give up control because you're not.

7. If you have children or are thinking about children, discuss your future financial goals for them. Are you thinking of private education and university or kicking them out when they reach 18 years old? What about childcare? Can you afford to be a stay-at-home mum or do you want to have the choice to be one?

8. What about your retirement? Are you hoping to retire abroad on state benefits (if so, think again) or do you have a pension fund growing steadily?

FINANCIAL FREEDOM
MAKING AND SAVING MONEY

It's only by saving that you will give your finances a kick-start and also realise how much you actually spend on unnecessary purchases. Even if you only have a tiny bit to save each month, every little bit counts towards the greater picture.

1. Create wealth by saving

'Why save?', you may be asking. Well, apart from the fact that savings give you financial security, without them how are you ever going to put any of your future plans into action? Savings not only allow for a change in your financial circumstances (more common than you think) but also actually allow you to have the future you want.

So, think about your financial strategy. Ideally, you should have a financial portfolio that has both long-term (pension) and short-term (house and holiday) goals. Here's how to do it:

START SAVING
Ideally, you should save 10 per cent of what you earn each month. If that figure is too horrible to consider, then save what you can, no matter how small. The idea is to get used to saving and make it as big a part of you as spending.

SAVE AS MUCH AS YOU CAN

Studies show that most of us can save each month if we break it down in our minds. For example, £200/$200 a month is only £50/$50 a week, and just £7/$7 a day. Can you cut £7/$7 a day from your current budget?

BE A CONSCIOUS SHOPPER

Save money by shopping wisely. Shop on the Internet for cheaper bargains, buy during the sales (but only what you were genuinely looking for), and work on the basis that if you have three pairs of jeans you don't need one more. Know how much you're paying for your utilities, phone line, insurance and pension funds (yes, sometimes companies charge you an account fee to save!). By becoming aware of the money that's needlessly slipping through your fingers you can save it instead of losing it.

DIRECT DEBIT YOUR SAVINGS EACH MONTH

Saving can actually be as addictive as buying, once you watch the numbers soar upwards. If you don't trust yourself to save each month, take the decision out of your hands by direct-debiting your savings the moment you get paid. What's more, once you pay off your debt (and you will), take the £200/$200 you were paying each month and immediately dump it into your savings. You don't need it – you just spent X amount each month without it.

THINK LONG-TERM AND SHORT-TERM PORTFOLIOS

Ask any financial expert (or rich person) and they'll tell you they have a variety of savings based on short-term, mid-term and long-term goals. Long term should be a pension – for retirement – whereas mid-term is for a house, or getting fired. Short term should be for holidays, or for savings to buy a car, TV, a fancy outfit.

INVEST WISELY

Take measured risks; that is, risks you can afford. Although shares, bonds and unit trusts are good ways to make money, as tempting as it is to dabble in the stock market, you need to ask yourself whether you know what you are doing and whether you can afford to lose money. If not, always seek the advice of an independent broker before you buy shares.

INVEST IN A PROPERTY

This is still the best long-term investment you can make, as long as you don't over-borrow on your mortgage, borrow constantly against the value of the property, or hope to double your money in a year. Property makes money because it's an investment that grows and eventually makes you money. On average, aim to stay in your house for three to five years, and think location, location, location. Also, don't fool yourself into thinking you can turn a wreck into a palace (especially if you have no DIY skills or excess cash), or that you can get rich quick by buying in a country you know nothing about. Also, gone are the days when you'll get rich quick by buying and selling houses; although your property will still increase in value, this is a mid to long-term investment that will steadily grow in value for you.

2. What does financial security mean to you?

Wealth comes from what you don't spend, not from the size of your wage packet. Keep grumbling that 30k a year doesn't allow you to become financially secure, and it never will. If you want financial security, firstly ask yourself what it will take: a million in the bank? A house? No mortgage? No debt? The answer will be different for everyone, and only you can say what true security means to you.

One thing that you should be aware of is that no matter how little you may earn by saving on a regular basis, you can end up with a hefty bank balance. I know this from experience, because I was someone who used up any money I had left after rent and bills because I felt it was there to be used up. Then, one day, while shopping in a wealthy area of town, I bumped into an old friend who was a PA, and was surprised to hear that this woman, who earned a quarter of my salary, lived in a gorgeous house in the area.

It turned out that since the age of 18, while I had been spending up a storm on my credit cards, she had been putting away £100/$100 a month, and increasing this amount every time she got a pay rise or windfall. She'd then invested wisely and doubled her savings, so by the age of 33 she had been able to put down a sizeable deposit on the house of her dreams.

What's more, she hadn't deprived herself for years to do this but had simply been more disciplined than most. She'd read up on finances, asked experts for help, and educated herself in the art of good invest-ments, all with a future goal in mind.

If she can do it on a minimal salary so can you. Whatever your goal, seek out financial information to improve your financial know-how. This information is free in the financial section of newspapers, and on the Internet, or buy a book on the subject. All you have to do is make a decision to educate yourself and you can find the route to creating wealth for your future.

Have no idea where to start? Well, ask yourself this: am I living the way I want to, and, if not, what will I have to do to get me there?

'I am always juggling from day to day, paying one credit card off with the other, switching cards, getting loans, arguing for a larger overdraft. If I was solvent, I'd actually be a great financial adviser.'

SARAH, 28

TEN WAYS TO BREAK THE SPENDING HABIT

1. Work in cash so that you physically see the money you're handing over.

2. Take the thrill out of 'impulse buys'. When you see something you absolutely have to buy, leave the shop and consider the purchase overnight.

3. Rate all purchases on a want/have/need scale of 1–10. If you score 7 or below, don't buy it.

4. Before you buy anything, ask yourself, 'Do I really need another X.'

5. Don't shop with friends who encourage your spending.

6. Reconsider the word bargain – it's not a bargain if you didn't need it in the first place.

7. Don't shop when bored or depressed – spending won't make you feel better for more than half an hour.

8. Avoid shopping at weekends out of habit – find a new hobby instead, you'll be amazed at how much you save.

9. Don't be flattered into buying something by a sales assistant or an advert – remind yourself that you can't buy into a lifestyle.

10. Shop without your debit and credit cards.

The aim of the one-month planner is to take a step-by-step approach to sorting out your finances. The three financial rules for the month are:

1. **Incorporate each tip into your daily life until it becomes second nature.**

2. **Keep a daily financial record.**

3. **Work in cash.**

> I've learnt to be good with money just by paying attention to what I am doing. I saved £100 a year on my mobile and changed all my utility bills and saved about £500 a year. I also shop carefully and now that I pay attention I am amazed at the differences in price. Where once I used to be a reckless shopper I now get my thrills from bargain hunting – it's saved me hundreds. **ANNE, 31**

WEEK ONE

MONDAY
Cut up all your credit cards except one. This is your emergency card and should be kept at home, not in your purse. Buy a small notepad and start keeping a daily spending diary.

TUESDAY
Spend one hour opening and sorting all your statements, credit payments, loan statements and demands, and work out how much you owe.

WEDNESDAY
Draw up a budget of outgoings and incomings using the information from Tuesday.

THURSDAY
Work out a repayment plan to reduce all your debts within a set time period that is practical.

FRIDAY
Look at your spending diary and work out where you can start to make cutbacks. Make three cutback decisions that you can start tomorrow.

SATURDAY
Declutter your house and work out what to sell, what to give away and then work out how much money your entire surplus has cost you. Sell your excess items from your clearout on eBay or through a second-hand store or flea market.

SUNDAY
Work out what professional advice you need on your debts, and check out the Internet for advice of where to go, call and email for help.

WEEK TWO

MONDAY
Take out your allotted money for the week (this should be in your budget) and then leave your cash card at home and work only in cash.

TUESDAY
Do a big grocery shop that does not include ready meals but allows for breakfast and lunches that you can take in to work.

WEDNESDAY
Try not to spend anything all day apart from necessary purchases such as travel. The challenge is to get used to not spending.

THURSDAY
Cancel any direct debits or standing orders that you don't use or really need such as gym membership, DVDs direct, insurance policies that aren't necessary (not your pension).

FRIDAY
Look at your mobile phone tariff and work out if you can get a cheaper deal.

SATURDAY
Go shopping with friends, but before you buy anything ask yourself how much you really need it. Scale your purchase desire from 1–10; anything under 7 put back.

SUNDAY
Arrange for all your credit/loans debits to go out of your account on the day you get paid.

WEEK THREE

MONDAY
Look at your spending diary again and work out your weak zones – is it Friday nights at the pub? PMS urges? Clothes? Think about how you can deal with the root of the problem.

TUESDAY
Look at all your bills and work out the best way to pay them: direct debit each month (no good if your bills are small, because you're just giving money away), quarterly payments and/or if you're better off changing service providers to save money in the long term.

WEDNESDAY
Work out ways you can up your income. Is it worth taking another job to help pay off your debts, or looking for a new job?

THURSDAY
Think about your future objectives. Write down three things you want to own in the next five years. Now work out how you're going to make that happen.

1. _____
2. _____
3. _____

FRIDAY
Change your social habits. Don't buy rounds, stick to buying your own drinks, and eat before you go out – it will save you busting your budget on a meal out.

SATURDAY
Work out a list of social activities you can do that don't cost money, and ask your friends to help you stick to it. There's no shame in admitting you need to cut back.

SUNDAY
Find two new hobbies that don't cost money but get you out of the house.

WEEK FOUR

MONDAY
Think about how much you can save – any amount counts even if it's under £50/$50. The challenge is to get used to putting money aside.

TUESDAY
Open a savings plan and direct debit the above amount into it each month on the day you get paid.

WEDNESDAY
If you don't have a retirement fund (pension) think about getting one.

THURSDAY
Be gift conscious. Don't be too generous – give within your means and plan ahead for gifts you may have to buy.

FRIDAY
If you've fallen off the financial wagon – or let certain areas slip – don't give up, just give yourself a financial shake-up. Climb back on again and re-budget, taking into account your blow-outs.

SATURDAY
Plan a trip for the summer within your new budget and start putting money aside each week.

SUNDAY
Give yourself a treat (within your budget) you deserve it – you're on your way to being a new financial whiz.

Relationships

Introduction

Whether you're madly in love, searching madly for it or madly trying to extricate yourself from someone, one thing is for sure: relationships are a major part of our lives. Meaning, they tend to affect everything from how we live today, to our future plans and even our day-to-day finances. Of course, if you're single you are probably reading this and thinking: I don't care about all that, I just want a partner. If so, it's worth noting that being in love isn't always the key to a happy life full of optimism.

It's a bitter pill to swallow, but relationships are often hard to maintain, and even good ones take time, effort and lots of compromise to ensure they work. This is simply because having two people agree to merge their views, life experiences, pasts and future aims into one solitary path takes maximum effort. Of course, if you are lucky, your Mr Perfect will have the same outlook as you, but love isn't always so easy.

Ask anyone who's got a failed relationship behind them and you'll hear a story loaded with insecurity, heartbreak and betrayals, as well as bizarre behaviour and out-of-character actions. I know this myself, as there have been times where I have been a class A bunny boiler, tracking down a boyfriend's every move and pestering him with pathetic 'I need you' texts. And at other times I've been on the other side of someone else's needy behaviour. I've also been single for a long period of time, when I thought that I wanted love but then rejected dates over ridiculous things like the drinks they ordered at the bar or the way they wore their hair. I've also been in love and been lucky enough to meet someone who loves me in return in the same way.

The good news is my story is not unusual. For 99.9 per cent of us there is someone out there who's Mr Right (or Mrs Right), and, for those currently in a relationship that is flagging, causing unhappiness and breaking at the seams, there is a way to sort out your problems. It all starts by taking a long, hard look at what you want and why. It's no good just saying, 'I want to be in love', because the reality is you want to be loved and love someone back, and you want that to be someone who not only appreciates you but also sticks by you when times are tough. This means that, like any other part of your life – be that finances, career, and even your body – making it through means honing your skills: your communication skills, your listening skills, your flirting skills and your loving skills. Do all of these and you're halfway to changing your relationships for the better.

So, whether it's heartbreak or the realisation that you need a helping hand that has brought you to this section, here's how to uncover the new relationship you.

Quiz

WHAT'S YOUR LOVE TYPE?

Understanding what you need from a relationship and how you act
when you're in one will give you a better idea about how to make your
relationships work. The following quiz and exercises are designed to give
you a clearer insight into your attitude to your love life. Go with your gut
feeling when answering, then look at the next page for the results.

1. **If you were single would you ever consider applying to a
   personal ad?**
   a. No – it smacks of desperation. **(HM)**
   b. No, real love doesn't happen like that. **(D)**
   c. Yes – it's a numbers game; you've got to be in it to win it. **(T)**
   d. You've already tried it plenty of times. **(P)**

2. **Every time you fall in love you think:**
   a. I've met my soul mate. **(D)**
   b. We're getting married. **(HM)**
   c. I wonder how long this will last. **(T)**
   d. I'm bored. **(P)**

3. **When you argue with your partner you think:**
   a. Oh no, this is the end. **(HM)**
   b. We're not right for each other. **(D)**
   c. I hate fighting; it makes me feel insecure. **(T)**
   d. I don't need this hassle. **(P)**

4. **Do you believe in the idea of 'The One'?**
   a. No – there are lots of Mr Rights out there. **(T)**
   b. No – because experience tells you otherwise. **(P)**
   c. Yes – absolutely, you're waiting for him. **(D)**
   d. Only when you're in love. **(HM)**

5. **Who's your ideal partner?**
   a. Someone handsome, fit and rich. **(HM)**
   b. A partner who is like you. **(T)**
   c. A partner who is your opposite. **(P)**
   d. You don't know but you know he's out there. **(D)**

6. **Post-honeymoon period you usually:**
   a. Fall out of love with someone. **(D)**
   b. Leave. **(P)**
   c. Feel more secure. **(T)**
   d. Get needy and demanding. **(HM)**

7. **The last break-up you went through was due to:**
   a. Wanting different things. **(T)**
   b. An affair. **(P)**
   c. Not being appreciated enough. **(HM)**
   d. You have no idea. **(D)**

8. **When a man doesn't ring when he says, you assume he's:**
   a. Lost your number. **(D)**
   b. Out with another woman. **(P)**
   c. Forgotten about you. **(HM)**
   d. A loser. **(T)**

Results

Add up all the answers you gave that were followed by (D) and then those followed by (T), and so on. Then see which score was the highest. If you scored highest on the (D) answers that makes you a Dreamer, see below. If you scored highest on the (T) answers that makes you a Thinker, and so on.

DREAMER (D)

You're in search of a soul mate who will make all your dreams come true, and maybe you are also just a little bit in love with the idea of love. While this is very romantic, it's worth knowing romance can sometimes be the enemy of love. Meaning, it's a good way to avoid being in love. However, the good news is that if you take off those love-tinted glasses, it won't take you long to find the love you need (rather than want). Just remember: no person is 100 per cent perfect, and no one can just adore you all the time. If you're in a relationship, it can also help to lower your expectations of what love can do for your life. Love can't erase your hang-ups or financial problems, or even make you feel happy if you're not already. Don't lay responsibility for your life on someone else, and reject him or her when they don't live up to your ideal.

THINKER (T)

Although you look before you leap and are very wary of making rash relationship moves, when you do fall in love you are a loyal and devoted partner. But, the problem is, if your partner lets you down then it's good-bye to him, as you're very black and white about love. This vision can cause havoc in your relationships, as it means that there is no room for forgiveness, manoeuvre or growth. You need to accept that love is sometimes a messy journey, as this will give you (and your partner) a break when things go awry. If you're single you need to watch that you don't think yourself out of a relationship by over-analysing someone's behaviour. Give yourself time to see if you like someone, and follow your gut instinct, but don't over-analyse their words, actions and dress sense – sometimes it pays to trust your heart not your head.

HIGH MAINTENANCE (HM)

You're a whirlwind in love, a force that can seem callous to those left behind. You demand a lot from the person you're with, and sometimes it can seem to your lovers that this relationship is all about you. Although it's good to know what you want, for a relationship to work you should also listen to your partner's needs. Love is a two-way process, and it's easy for one person to fall into the shadow of another and simply be labelled the giver, which in the long term is a recipe for disaster, as it means the relationship can only grow so far. If you're keen to stick to your high-maintenance requirements, make sure you always give as much as you take; otherwise, all your relationships are going to have a natural sell-by date.

PLAYER (P)

To friends you act as if you don't mind short-term affairs, one-night stands and being single, but there's a part of you that craves long-term love and security but does everything to avoid it. To create intimacy in your relationships, you need to (1) allow someone to like you for yourself; that is, show them who you really are, by being 'real' with them; and (2) learn how to trust both your partner and yourself. If you've been a player for a while this can be hard, as we tend to judge others by our own actions. So, if you've cheated on someone and got bored in the past, then you assume that others will do this, too. To break the cycle you need to look at where your distrust and desire to play the field comes from and tackle these issues before you tackle love.

RELATIONSHIP THERAPY

WHAT DOES LOVE MEAN TO YOU?

What can you do to improve your relationship? What is love and what does it mean to you? For some people, love is the illicit thrill of meeting someone new and wanting to rip off their clothes. For others, it's hearts, roses, and candlelit dinners, and for others still, it's the meeting of someone who knows you inside out. Relationships, on the other hand, are a different kettle of fish. They can be infuriating, exciting, happy, miserable, compromising, or all of these things and more. When I was younger, love and relationships meant exciting thrills and much fantasy-style yearning. My first experience of love was a crush on a pop star who wore make-up, and couldn't sing. Later I transferred my affection to the boy everyone loved at school; the boy who didn't even know my name, and yet, the boy I spent months yearning after. Later, my choices were even more inappropriate: the cheating college boy, the alcoholic 'don't-worry-I-can-handle-it' guy, the fickle 'I-want-to-be-a-pop-star' man – who still happens to be a waiter – and the blond surf boy with druggie tendencies and a good line in lies.

I've also dated a man who offered to buy me a sports car, others who wrote me songs and some who just wouldn't leave me alone long after we broke up. Through it all I swore I was enjoying it, even though it often left me in one of three states: (1) crying; (2) saying 'why me?'; or (3) doing (1) and (2) at the same time.

Despite my obviously flawed approach to loving, I kept going back for more, not because I was a sucker for punishment but because I now realise I secretly liked the sensation of being taken up by a force bigger than myself; although obviously not the part where I was then dropped from a great height. As a result it took me a long time to see the light and wake up to myself.

These days love means something completely different. It's something that makes me laugh, makes me silly and, above all, makes me happy. Gone are the bracing highs of will-he-won't-he call, but, thankfully, also gone is the misery of being trapped in a relationship that's clearly not working. To get here I didn't just get lucky and meet someone who was right for me – I had to stop and take a long, hard look at my relationship decisions. No one ends up in a terrible relationship out of bad luck, it's always a combination of bad choices that gets you to a point where things start to crack. Of course, sometimes it's definitely the other person's fault, and sometimes it's yours, but it takes action to change things. So the question is: what does your relationship say about your decisions and what can you start doing to make yourself happy? Read on and find out.

STEP ONE:

WARNING – is your love life in distress?

You may be thinking: what love life? In which case, you are definitely in relationship distress. Signs you're also heading for the relationship counsellor's couch include unspoken resentment, anger issues that can't be resolved, a sex life you're unhappy with and not being able to look at your partner without feeling sick to the stomach. If you're single, your love life is in distress if you write off all your dates after one meeting, refuse even to go on a date, and have a deeper relationship with your remote control than the outside world.

So here's the first piece of advice: love is not a passive emotion. Love is not something that just happens to you, and the state of your love life will not get better if you just sit back and hope. In order to change your love life, action needs to be taken. And this means breaking down your relationship problems into workable areas so that you can see them for what they are. Up until now you may have avoided this path simply because you know that once you uncover your issues you have no choice but to act on them – but the good news is: the only way is up.

If you are in a relationship, work out what is distressing you by asking yourself:

1. **Is it your partner's actions? How do these make you feel?**
2. **Is it the expectations you have about your relationship? What are these expectations?**
3. **Do you both have differing goals? If so, what do you want, or what does your partner want?**
4. **Do you feel taken for granted? In what areas do you feel resentful?**
5. **Is it the state of your sex life? How could things be improved?**
6. **Do you feel that you are not heard by your partner? In what ways do you feel you are not heard?**

If you are single, work out what is distressing you by asking yourself:

1. **Is it because you have a succession of bad dates?**
2. **Do you feel that your dates are a disaster? In what ways are they disastrous?**
3. **Do you feel that the men who you like never call you back? How proactive are you about taking the next step?**
4. **Are you unable to get over an ex? What's stopping you?**
5. **Do you feel ashamed that you're single? What's wrong with waiting for the right person to come along?**
6. **Are you under pressure from friends and family to find a partner? How could you reassure them you are fine?**

The problem with being single, or in a relationship that's going through a rocky patch, is that everyone has got an opinion about why things are going wrong. When I was single I had friends telling me, 'You're too fussy', my parents saying, 'You'll get stuck in your ways', and even dates informing me that the reason I was alone was because I was 'too sharp/too funny' and even 'too clever' for men. Now I'm in a relationship, the same people have equally annoying things to add to our ups and downs. The point here being, that at the end of the day only you can work out the answers to your relationship glitches, so don't let others interfere.

Start by looking at the ways you choose to cope with your current love life.

EXERCISE ONE

List three ways to make yourself feel better about your current love life:

_____   _____   _____

Looking at your answers, ask yourself: do your coping mechanisms really make you feel better, or are they avoidance tactics that give you an excuse not to try to change things?

Theories aside, what do you think is the one thing holding you back from having a successful relationship? What would it take to make you do something drastic to revive or fix your love life?

Now list three reasons why you keep on doing what you're doing.

a. _____

b. _____

c. _____

Remember: no one ever does something that doesn't repay him or her with some kind of positive return, so work out what you're getting from your behaviour. For example, if you're single and have given up dating because you're certain there are no good men left, could it be that you're doing this to save yourself from being hurt and/or feeling rejected or despondent?

If you're in a relationship where all you do is bicker, are you doing this as a way of avoiding your bigger and potentially more dangerous issues or because it's become a comfortable habit?

STEP TWO:

Your love profile/map

How we love and just who we choose to fall in love with doesn't happen by chance, it's the direct result of our personal love maps. This, say the experts, is the blueprint we carry for our ideal relationship — a psychological map that has been formed by attitudes and experiences from our lives. This is why to change your relationship for the better you first have to look at where your beliefs and expectations came from. Relationship counsellors now believe the past manifests itself in hidden expectations and assumptions that end up sabotaging our love lives. If you feel constantly disappointed, betrayed and let down by love, the chances are your hidden and known expectations haven't been met time and time again.

To discover what makes up your love map, think back and recall the memories you have about how your parents loved, communicated and got on. These are important because although they may not be how you think and act in relationships, they are the foundations of how you came to your conclusions about love and marriage. Do you remember your parents consistently criticising each other? Or perhaps you lived in a house where everyone was very polite and never said what was on their mind, or maybe your family was one where love was overly expressed or withheld. Your attitude to relationships today is likely to be either a replica of one of your parents' views or the opposite of how you were brought up.

To help uncover the past, write down:

1. **What positive and negative messages were you given about relationships and love when growing up?**

2. **How did your parents treat each other?**

3. **How did your parents resolve arguments?**

4. **How happy were your parents in your eyes?**

Looking at how your parents reacted to their problems can help you to uncover the basis for yours. Take Sarah, 35, her four-year relationship was heading for ruin over endless fights that her partner took her for granted:

'Everything Matt did, whether it was leaving washing-up in the sink, asking me to pick up his dry-cleaning or simply leaving dirty towels on the floor, would throw me into a fury. In his eyes he couldn't see that the problem was that big, but in my eyes I felt taken for granted and belittled by his behaviour. Then, I was moaning to my mum one day and she laughed and said, "Oh your dad still does that", and I suddenly realised that I'd grown up watching my mum basically be my dad's slave without a word of complaint, and it had driven me mad that she never spoke up for herself. It hasn't cured our domestic problems, but I am calmer and more rational about the issue now. I see his slovenly housekeeping skills as a laziness problem rather than a sign that he wants me to wait on him.'

EXERCISE TWO

1. Does the way you love and behave in relationships reflect your mother's behaviour, or your father's, or neither?
2. List two beliefs you hold about relationships and men.

   a. _____

   b. _____

3. List two beliefs you hold about relationships and women.

   a. _____

   b. _____

Your relationship beliefs and expectations are only ideas that you've emphasised to yourself, which means you can change them by simply deciding to. For example, are you secretly hoping that your current partner will make up for previous hurts in your life, and does this belief get shaken every time you have a fight or he lets you down? If so, you need to challenge your belief about dealing with your past issues and not put the onus on your partner.

Similarly, if you're hoping that one day you'll meet Mr Right and feel loved, happy and fulfilled in every way, it's likely that a bad date has rocked your confidence about the whole of your life. If so, you need to keep the experience in perspective. It was a date, it was bad, but that doesn't automatically mean a life alone is forever on the cards.

Expectation 1	I want my partner to know what I want without having to tell him or her.
Solution	You need to start saying what you want and need. No one can be a mind-reader no matter how well they know and love you; expecting them to be able to is a way of sabotaging your relationship.
Expectation 2	If we were right for each other we would never argue.
Solution	Arguments are an unavoidable part of two different people getting together. It's part of the process of how we mesh our lives together. Everyone argues, and to think that you're the only ones who ever do is a way to destroy your relationship.
Expectation 3	If he found me attractive he would want sex with me all the time.
Solution	No one (not even you) wants sex all the time, especially when life gets in the way. If you're feeling rejected, work out if you want the actual sex, or whether you want the reassurance that your partner finds you attractive.
Expectation 4	If I was thinner/prettier/smarter I would have a boyfriend.
Solution	There are plenty of girls who disprove the above theories about relationships. Meeting someone is not about who you are and what you look like, but about how many people you get out there and meet. As the old saying goes: it's a numbers game.

Expectation 5	**I deserve to meet Mr Right after all I've been through.**
Solution	**This may be true, but wishing alone does not make things happen. Being proactive and not self-pitying is what will get you your relationship.**
Expectation 6	**My next relationship will be my serious one.**
Solution	**Whereas it's good to know if you and another person are heading in the same direction, don't put pressure on yourself or a new partner by pushing your relationship too far too soon just because you're tired of dating. Instead, live for the moment and see where that takes you first.**

STEP THREE:

Look at your relationship history

In the same way that no one wants to be judged on the behaviour of their friends, you shouldn't really judge anyone on their ex-partners, because we all have at least one dating mishap in our pasts. The power of dating is that it helps us redefine and discover who we want to be with. It's an important process because, often, who we think we want to be with is more of a projection of who we want to be, or the life we want to lead, rather than what we really need.

So, if you're always falling for people who are wrong for you, or are currently in a relationship where history seems to be repeating itself, it pays to look at your past. The first thing to realise is that the past doesn't have to equal the future unless you let it. If you've had a traumatic and painful childhood, been in an abusive relationship, or any number of other things that now ensure you arrive in relationships with masses of emotional baggage, do something about it. Whether that means getting professional help, seeking the advice of an expert or letting go, only you can say. If you don't, it will continue to affect your current relationship status and your emotional choices.

We go out with people who are 'bad' for us for a number of reasons. If you've done it many, many times it's not because you're a sucker for punishment but because in a strange way it's probably comfortable. For a long time I dated a whole host of losers simply because I knew what I was getting.

It was also easier to be with them and say, 'If only he wasn't druggie/alcoholic/womaniser/idiot' then we'd be really happy, than find someone who challenged me to get out of my comfort zone, be real and have a loving relationship. My bad relationships were, therefore, the direct result of bad decisions, such as not fol-lowing my gut instincts and willingly putting up with ridiculous behaviour, rather than simple bad luck.

EXERCISE THREE

1. Look back over your relationship history and work out if there's a clear type of person you've been going for.

2. What did you get from these relationships? If you're unsure, see below, which lists some of the reasons why we're attracted to certain personality types.

IF YOU ALWAYS FALL FOR MEN WHO 'NEED' YOU

You're suffering from Florence Nightingale syndrome and have a deep need to 'fix' other people's lives. This is usually rooted in childhood – look back and identify what it is that makes you want to rescue others over yourself.

IF YOU ALWAYS FALL FOR PEOPLE WHO ARE ATTACHED

If you've had a host of married or attached lovers, the chances are you get an ego boost knowing you can tempt them away from their wife or partner. If you want a relationship that works with real intimacy, choose men who are not looking for thrills on the side. This means raising your standards and opting for guys who are available and looking for love.

IF YOU ALWAYS FALL FOR THE BAD GUY

You're stuck in a teenage mindset where the 'bad' guy is always more exciting, sexy and thrilling to be with. Could it be that you're dating 'bad' boys because it's a way to find your bad side? Break the habit by thinking about what these guys are not bringing to your relationship table.

IF YOU ALWAYS GO FOR THE PERSON WHO PLACES YOU ON A PEDESTAL

This is a low self-esteem issue. If you always choose men who think you're perfect, it's akin to having your own cheerleading squad on hand 24 hours a day. The only problem is your time on that pedestal is limited, as you know, and once you fall off you either have to move on or face the real you.

IF YOU ALWAYS GO FOR THE VIOLENT PERSON

Finding yourself with a violent person can often be bad luck, as most violent men are very good at hiding their violent traits in the beginning. However, if you always end up with violent men you need to stop telling yourself you can help them, or stop taking the blame and seek professional help as soon as possible.

STEP FOUR:

Give love a chance

To give love a chance you have to be honest about what you want, what you need and what you give in a relationship. This is because relationship problems are rarely one-sided, so if your current relationship is going wrong, you need to work out what's keeping you in this relationship state (if you're single, base these questions on your last relationship). Write your answers in a notebook.

EXERCISE FOUR

1. Make three statements about your compatibility (or lack of it) with your partner.
2. Take each statement and ask yourself how true each of them is (we often keep telling ourselves things that no longer hold true out of habit).
3. What does/or did your gut instinct tell you about your present/last relationship?
4. If you followed your gut instinct today, what two actions would you immediately take to change your love status?

Example: Anna, 30, is in a relationship with James, 32.

In the last two years she has been supporting him, as he wants to be in a band. Anna supported her last two boyfriends as well, one who was a writer and another who wanted to change careers. Anna and James have a baby on the way, and Anna keeps hoping that this will stir James into taking part of the financial burden and getting a job. She is six months pregnant and so far nothing has happened on the work front.

1. **Make three statements about your compatibility (or lack of it) with your partner.**

   a. He has real talent and I love that he knows what he wants to do and is willing to go for it.
   b. We have a good relationship where we can talk about anything
   c. I love him.

2. **Take each statement and ask yourself how true each of them is (we often keep telling ourselves things that no longer hold true out of habit).**

   a. I secretly believe he's too old to make it in a band now, and it annoys me that he can't be realistic.
   b. We can't talk about everything because I want him to step up and take some of the financial burden without me having to ask him to do this.
   c. I do love him.

3. What does/ or did your gut instinct tell you about your present/ last relationship?

That if James doesn't get a job before the baby comes I am going to become resentful and, eventually, angry.

4. If you followed your gut instinct today, what two actions would you immediately take to change your love status?

I'd tell him my fears and ask him to start contributing towards the bills and mortgage.

TWELVE WAYS NOT TO GIVE LOVE A CHANCE

Aside from your problems there are plenty more ways not to give love a chance. Work out which ones feel true for you, and consciously do something positive about them.

1. **Being overly critical.**
2. **Wanting more than you give.**
3. **Picking on your partner all the time.**
4. **Not being honest about your feelings.**
5. **Not giving new men a chance.**
6. **Projecting what you want on to others.**
7. **Making generalisations about men, women and love.**
8. **Always pushing for what you want.**
9. **Not listening.**
10. **Not saying what you need.**
11. **Telling yourself you're bad at loving.**
12. **Believing you're not lovable.**

RELATIONSHIP REHAB
STARTING AGAIN

It's not over until it's over, as the old saying goes, which means you can start again at any time – and this means start dating again, start a new relationship or even start again within your present relationship. By now you've hopefully highlighted the reasons why you feel unhappy about relationships, so it's time to put what you know into practice. Firstly, it's worth knowing that whenever you get together with someone, problems are unavoidable, because, no matter how alike you are, each of you came to the relationship with two sets of opinions of how things should be done, two sets of beliefs and two sets of expectations. Meshing these happily together takes effort, compromise and work.

Secondly, if you're very unhappy in love right now, or unhappy about your love life, it's likely you feel disappointed and maybe even betrayed because either something you expected to happen hasn't or something you enjoyed has stopped happening. To start the process of making the above change you need to take action. So, take a notebook and start by writing a list of five things you want/need to rectify in your present love life.

IF YOU'RE IN A RELATIONSHIP, THESE COULD BE:

- Your attitude ....
- Communication ....
- Sex life ....
- Mutual goals ....
- Domestic arrangements ....

And if you're single:

- Meet new people ....
- Try new dating avenues ....
- Practise your flirting skills ....
- Being happily single ....
- Choosing appropriate partners ....

Beside each point, write one way you can achieve this today.

IF YOU'RE IN A RELATIONSHIP

Sort out your attitude and change from negative to positive

Practise putting a positive twist on your problems.

Improve communication

Practise five minutes of active listening three times today – this is where you don't interrupt while your partner is speaking.

Sort out your sex life

Go on a date and come up with a compromise between what you want and what he wants.

Find a direction that you are both willing to go in

Discuss future goals together on a date. Brainstorm and make it fun, rather than a rehash session of your problems.

Negotiate petty arguments

Discuss these outside the heat of the moment, and have a ten-minute 'time out' period to cool down.

IF YOU'RE SINGLE

Make more effort to meet new people

Say yes to all the invites that come your way and don't give yourself a get-out clause.

Try new dating avenues

Call up all your best friends and ask them to set you up with someone. It's not a sign of desperation but a sign of being proactive.

Practise your flirting skills

Try being charming with waiters, shop assistants and anyone else you meet today.

Work on being happily single

Forget love for a moment and come up with financial, career and body goals to boost your self-esteem.

Choose appropriate men

Practise following your gut instinct when you meet new men (any men, not just potential dates). What does your gut feeling tell you about them? Are you right?

Ensure that you put into practice at least three actions today.

1. Finding love

Finding love isn't, of course, as easy as writing a love wish list, but for every woman who complains that she's tried and failed, the chances are she's not utilising all that she can. So, if you're currently looking for love, you need to first ask yourself what exactly you are looking for.

Choosing a partner should be 50 per cent knowing what you want and 50 per cent being open to new experience, which means you should at least have an idea of who you're looking for and why before you go out hunting, but not be too regimental about it.

To help yourself, complete the following:

I want a partner who is:

a._____

b._____

I want these things because:

a._____

b._____

These traits would suit my personality because:

_____

Places I could potentially find this type of person (brainstorm this part with friends):

a._____

b._____

c._____

What two new things can I do today to make me feel proactive about dating?

a._____

b._____

If, on the other hand, you are 100 per cent sure of what you want, you need to work out if it's your list that is stopping you from meeting someone. It's virtually impossible to find someone who'll hit every marker, and if you're unwilling to bend your views, you could well be missing out on relationships with people who could make you very happy indeed.

And don't be fooled; meeting a partner is definitely a numbers game. If you're someone who doesn't believe in looking for love (as in, opening yourself up to opportunities to meet someone) because you believe love has more to do with destiny, you're missing the point.

A numbers game doesn't mean dating hundreds of people, but simply going out and meeting lots and lots of new people so that you can widen your social circle. This is essential because (1) it gives you more opportunities; and (2) it potentially puts you into contact with hundreds of single people (think about each four new people you meet, knowing four more people, who know four more people, and so on). This then gives you a full pool to choose from.

Next, don't wait to be chosen – do the choosing. Not only is this more proactive and more fun but it also takes the sting out of dating because it puts you firmly in control.

To do the choosing ensure you:

- **Practise flirting.**

- **Take risks to move out of your comfort zone.**

- **Widen your dating avenues – think personals, dating groups, blind dates.**

- **Lose your romantic vision of 'the one' – there are lots of suitable people for you, not just one person who fits all.**

- **Have fun – that's the whole point of dating.**

2. Keeping love

The biggest problem with arguing with a loved one is the gap between how you see yourself and how they see you. For example, you may think you're straightforward, good at communication and clear about your problems but your partner may register you as confrontational, bullying and prone to exaggeration. The trick is not always to insist you're right but consider if perhaps your partner has a point.

When arguing, it always pays to be:

- **Kind about the way you say things.**

- **More controlled about what you say.**

- **Less dramatic with emotions.**

- **Clearer about what's wrong.**

- **Firmer about what you're saying.**

- **More sure of what you need.**

- **Less accusatory when trying to problem-solve.**

What do you clash over? Is it money, domestic issues, sex or parenting? Whatever your major issues are, you have to face them in order to iron out your relationship problems.

Which of the following people are you like?

Anna, 36, who says, 'I feel huge resentment towards my husband. We both work, but when it comes to childcare, household duties and bills, I do it all. When we argue he says he believes he does his share, but the reality is he does a tenth of what I do and is unappreciative of that fact.'

Claire, 27, 'I feel my partner undermines me in front of friends and family, as he's always putting my job down and laughing about my abilities to better myself at college. When we try to discuss it he says I'm too sensitive, but I feel he's a bully.'

Sam, 28, 'We both hate confrontation, so we tend to gloss over our problems. I'm not happy with our sex life but I could never tell my boyfriend this; it would hurt him terribly, but then post-sex I always feel let down and frustrated and end up bickering with him about something that really isn't his fault.'

Or are you someone who believes 'everything' is the problem. If so, you need to define what areas irk you the most. The best way to do this is to rate your irritation and frustration from 1 to 10 each time you feel it rising. For example, you're frustrated because your partner has left all the washing-up in the sink. If you rate your irritation above 5 this is about more than washing-up – do you feel taken for granted and treated like someone's house slave, or is this about something else entirely? Another example: your partner goes out for a drink with his friends, and you're left feeling angry. If you score above 5 you need to ask yourself why. Are you worried about money or do you feel you never get a night out? Or are you anxious about his behaviour when he's out without you or afraid of what he might do on the flirting front?

Instead of fighting about the issue, such as washing-up/going out, you need to discuss the feelings at the root of your irritation; that is, your fears that are being triggered by your clashes.

The best way to do this is to improve your communication skills. Unfortunately, when conflict arises this is the first area that goes to pot, mainly because we're all lousy listeners. We interrupt, misinterpret what we hear, and switch off when we register what sounds like criticism. To mend a relationship, you have to teach yourself to listen to your partner. Start by giving each other floor space, and then be sure not to speak while your partner is speaking. When they have finished, paraphrase what was said to reassure your partner that you've heard, and then say your piece. When you do this, focus not on defending yourself or retaliating but on repair work.

HOW TO COMMUNICATE

Tips for speaking:

- **Speak your mind. Don't ask your partner to be a mind-reader and don't make assumptions about what he/she believes.**
- **Keep your statements brief and to the point. Don't go on and on.**
- **Let your partner paraphrase what you're saying so that you're sure he or she has 'heard' you.**
- **Don't patronise/attack if you want a positive outcome.**

Tips for listening:

- **Don't interrupt – the speaker has the floor.**
- **Listen actively – don't just wait for your turn to say your piece.**
- **Paraphrase to ensure you've heard correctly.**
- **Pay attention – don't let your mind drift.**

Above all, if you're trying to save your relationship, be ready to compromise. Somewhere between what you both want is a middle ground, and you can reach it if you remember what is at stake. So, before you throw yourself into a discussion, know the outcome. This doesn't mean second-guess his moves, or try to outmanoeuvre him, but know what you want to happen here. What would be the best outcome in your eyes? What would leave you feeling the most content with the situation? What's your best compromise? And always remember this isn't about winning points or getting your way, it's about problem solving.

3. Leaving love

After you have addressed all of the above questions and techniques, you may of course come to a point where you feel there is no more hope for the two of you, because no matter what you do things don't get better. Once, when I was very unhappy in a relationship, I asked my best friend when I would know it was time to leave, and she wisely said, 'When you're more unhappy than happy', and she was right. Your feelings are the best indicator of whether or not things can go on. Other indicators, according to relationship experts, are as follows:

Indicators that all is not lost:
- **You still love each other.**
- **You still respect each other.**
- **You still want things to work out.**
- **You are both willing to work at your problems.**
- **You see your future with him.**

Indicators that it's time to leave
- **One of you has betrayed the other and the other can't get over it.**
- **Honesty and respect have gone.**
- **You feel contempt for your partner.**
- **You have given up even talking or arguing (also known as stone-walling).**
- **You can see your life without him in it.**

If you've reached the point where you really can't go on, what you need to do is ask yourself what's the best and cleanest way to extricate yourself from the relationship. If you're someone who needs 'closure', that is, needs to know exactly why things have fallen apart, be wary of giving your partner a list of his failings. Apart from ensuring weeks of acrimony, it's a guaranteed way not to get the very thing you're seeking. And remember: while you may have decided enough is enough, your partner may not be on the same page as you. Meaning, you may not be able to extricate yourself as easily as you would like, so be clear about your objectives right from the beginning.

You need to know:

1. **What plan of action you're going to follow for the break-up.**
2. **The reasons why you're ending things.**
3. **What needs to happen now between you and your ex.**

When breaking up, it's easy to let guilt get the better of you, so be strong and remember not to:

- **Give your partner false hope.**
- **Insist on being best friends right away.**
- **Talk about seeing other people.**
- **Tell them how to feel about this.**
- **Make excuses such as, 'It's me, not you.'**

Finally, be clear about contact. Don't let them call you at all hours, send you endless emails and see you to 'talk things over'. Boundaries are essential when you break up, for your sanity as well as theirs.

RELATIONSHIP FREEDOM
FINDING THAT FORMULA

Knowing what a healthy relationship is can help when you're stuck in one that's problematic. In a nutshell, a good relationship is not always one where you're simply madly in love, it's a relationship that leaves you feeling good about yourself and has you wanting to make someone else feel good, too. It's about good communication, good times and a sex life you're both happy with. To help yourselves keep your relationship on the right path ensure that you:

1. Learn to think as a couple

This doesn't mean turn into one person, but rather consider each other before you make decisions that affect each other. For example, where you live and work has an impact on your relationship, as does changing careers, wanting a baby and even, sometimes, going on holiday. To make things work, start thinking of yourself as only part of the decision process.

2. Have a life of your own

So you love being together and doing things together all the time, but it also pays to have your own life as well. Firstly, because

independence brings the rewards of self-esteem and self-confidence
that will benefit your relationship, and secondly, having a life outside of
each other is healthier than spending all your hours together.

3. Be honest about your objectives

Make sure you're both heading in the same direction. Don't just
assume your partner wants the same things as you, whether this is
marriage and kids, early retirement or a life abroad. Make sure you
talk regularly about where you're heading and where you see yourself
in the future. This doesn't mean make concrete plans but that you
are at least on the same page.

4. Be honest about your problems

Don't expect your partner to be a mind-reader or someone who
pretends everything is OK when it's so obviously not. You can work
through your problems only by being honest and open about them.
This means you need to talk about your fears, admit to insecurities
that are affecting your relationship and, above all, be willing to work
on issues that present themselves, whether they are coming from
you or your partner.

THE TEN MAIN INGREDIENTS FOR A SUCCESSFUL RELATIONSHIP

1. Mutual attractiveness – you find each other sexually attractive.

2. Enthusiasm – you're enthusiastic about each other and your relationship.

3. Affection – you kiss outside of sex.

4. Communication – you know how to speak to each other.

5. Honesty – you say what's on your mind.

6. Compatibility – you want the same things and understand where the other person is coming from.

7. Kindness – you're kind to each other when things go wrong.

8. Laughter – you are able to laugh over problems and mishaps.

9. Mutual morals – you have the same ideas about what's right and what's wrong.

10. Mutual direction – you know where you're both heading.

One-month Relationship Makeover

The aim of the one-month planner is to take a step-by-step approach to changing your relationships for the better. Work on building your day-by-day skills by taking 30 minutes out a day to think purely about improving your relationship. If you're single, use your last relationship as a basis for some of the tasks. Use your notebook to record your answers.

> **I thought I was the one always destined to be unlucky in love. Then I realised destiny had nothing to do with it — my own bad choices did. It sounds obvious but it was enlightening and changed everything.**
>
> **LUCY, 29**

WEEK ONE

MONDAY

Ask yourself just what's making you unhappy in your love life. Be specific, not vague, with your answers. If you're stuck, imagine your perfect romantic day with your partner. What elements are different in that day from the life you are living right now?

TUESDAY

Discover what you want from your relationship by listing all your hopes and expectations. Look at the list, and next to each hope rate from 1–10 how realistic these expectations are, and then rate how well they are being met.

WEDNESDAY

What are your partner's relationship expectations? Ask him to list and rate them as above. Then discuss your lists without attributing blame. The aim is to see where you're both coming from.

THURSDAY

Think about what's frustrating you the most. Is it lack of communication, too much analysis or not enough fun? If you're single, could it be that you can't find a decent partner or feel too old to date? Challenge your frustrations – what can you do to change this situation?

FRIDAY

Take a trip into the past – how much old baggage are you bringing into your present without realising it? What is your parents' relationship like and how about your partner's parents?

SATURDAY

Lighten up and go on a date. Make it something out of the ordinary – a special occasion just for the sake of it – and start making this a regular weekly occurrence. If you're single, do something daring to shake yourself out of your comfort zone.

SUNDAY

Thinking about your date last night, what went right and what went wrong? Are you repeating old patterns all the time? If you had fun, what changed the night for the better?

WEEK TWO

MONDAY
Spend time working out your love profile. What personality traits make up your perfect partner? The aim of this exercise is to help you focus on what makes you happy and what you put up with out of habit.

TUESDAY
List the contradictory expectations you impose on your partner (and the ones he imposes on you). Then come up with an action plan on how to change these expectations; start by asking for what you need.

WEDNESDAY
Consider whether you and your partner are playing the 'change game', that is, you're both trying to change each other subtly without realising it. Remember: it's impossible to change someone; you can only change your response to them.

THURSDAY
Reboot your sex life. If sex has gone off the boil ask yourself why. Is it low self-esteem, general relationship unhappiness or maybe even boredom that's turned your good sex life bad? Whatever the problem, do three positive things today to work towards a change in your sex life.

FRIDAY
Ask your partner to arrange this week's date, and let him sort everything out (don't be tempted to take over). Go along with whatever he decides. If you're single again, try a new avenue that you're afraid of: personal ads, blind dating or even speed dating.

SATURDAY
Did last night's date leave you feeling let down or happy? What went wrong and what went right?

SUNDAY
Aim to spend the whole day with each other without bickering or fighting. At the end of the day work out how well you did. If you're single, spend the day practising your flirting skills, and at the end rate your success on positive feedback.

WEEK THREE

MONDAY
Be consciously more loving and affectionate towards your partner (or friends and family) – it will improve intimacy and communication.

TUESDAY
Say what's on your mind. Don't let your partner have to second-guess you. This is not an open invitation to criticise or moan but to say what's bothering you and what your partner can do to help.

WEDNESDAY
Practise listening attentively with your work colleagues, friends, family and partner. Ask for feedback on how people felt when you listened to them.

THURSDAY
Have more fun together – forget about the serious stuff. What do you and your partner do consciously to have a good time together? If the answer is nothing, come up with a plan to change this. If you're single and not having fun, come up with a game plan that ups your social life.

FRIDAY
Talk about your perfect date and plan it together right down to the last detail. If you're single, get together with a group of single girlfriends and come up with a night out that allows you all to practise your flirting skills.

SATURDAY
Work out what's changed for the better between you so far. What areas still need work? If your plans have all gone wrong, is it the result of your goals or a sign that your relationship has deeper problems?

SUNDAY
Make a new life plan together. Take time out during the day together and sit down and brainstorm ideas for where you would like your life to go in the next five years. Work out where you would like to live, and what lifestyle you'd like to have together.

WEEK FOUR

MONDAY

Bring up the biggest issue that's bothering you. Tip: if you're the one who is speaking, keep your statements brief and to the point. Don't be tempted to go off on a tangent or list all the things your partner does that annoy you. Then let your partner paraphrase what you're saying so that you're sure he or she has 'heard' you correctly.

TUESDAY

Listen to your partner's biggest issue. How does hearing the problem your partner has with you make you feel? Overcome the urge to be defensive or retaliate, and together come up with two ways to start rectifying things.

WEDNESDAY

Don't undermine each other by bringing up the past when things get tough. It's rarely one person's fault when things start going wrong, so if you want to improve your relationship start with a clean slate and work forwards.

THURSDAY

Think about your own life. Are all your needs focused on your relationship? If so, you need to think about your own life, whether single or attached you should be doing things for yourself as well as others. Make two new personal goals today.

FRIDAY

Cover areas of your life that cause friction in your relationship such as money or parenting. How can you both work together on this? What issues drive you apart? What are your common aims in this area?

SATURDAY

What new skills could you and your partner learn to make your relationship work even better? Think laterally about how to incorporate these into your life; for example, if you need to learn teamwork, think about learning a new sport.

SUNDAY

Have a day date – a whole day where you get to live the perfect romantic day that you listed at the beginning of the month. If your single aim is to have a day that's just about you, for one day treat yourself and do exactly what you want.

Glossary

BODY

Aerobic exercise: This is exercise that requires oxygen and so raises the heart rate. It also improves lung capacity and burns fat.

Anaerobic: Exercise that doesn't require oxygen, this usually occurs during fast or hard bursts of exercise like weightlifting.

Calorie: The unit for measuring the energy value of food.

Carbohydrates: Foods, such as bread, whole grains, pasta, and fruit and vegetables, which are used as a fuel source for the body.

Heart rate: The level at which your heart has to pump in order to circulate blood around your body. The harder you exercise, the stronger the heart gets and the more blood it can pump with less effort.

Interval training: An intense technique where you alternate repetitively between short bursts of high-intensity exercise and low-intensity exercise (to bring your heart rate down).

Metabolic rate: The rate at which your body burns calories for energy.

Protein: One of the main building blocks the body uses to make hormones, give you energy and build muscle. You need to eat at least 35g (1 1/4 oz) of protein a day.

Protein-only diets: Diets that focus on eating protein-only foods in order to kick-start something called ketosis, which is where the body begins breaking down everything to burn calories.

Refined foods: Foods that are no longer in their 'whole' state, and are pre-packaged, usually with added sugars, fats and white flours.

Resistance training: Working with weights or using your body weight as a force to work against.

Vitamins: Naturally occurring substances that are essential for a healthy body. The best way to get them is through your food intake because this aids their integration into the body and helps them to work effectively.

Yo-yo dieting: The process of losing and gaining weight in a repeated cycle.

CAREER

Brand image: How you see yourself in the job market.

Curriculum vitae (CV): A history of your working life.

Myers-Briggs: One of the big personality tests that large corporations use.

Networking: Building work contacts by meeting people in the same industry as you.

Portfolio: Collection of work you have done – essential for creative jobs.

Psychometric testing: Tests that determine your reasoning and behaviour towards others.

Redundancy: Losing your job due to company downsizing, or your job becoming unessential.

Résumé: See CV.

Severance pay: Compensation in cash for a redundancy.

Skills: Abilities you are proficient in.

USP: Unique selling point – what you have that makes you unique in the market place.

FINANCE

Accountant: A person who prepares the financial records of a business or company.

ATM (automated teller machine): A machine for dispensing paper cash and confirming the balance you have in your bank account.

Bailiff: A person who has the power to seize property to the value of an unpaid debt.

Balance: The amount left over after money has been paid in and paid out of an account.

Bank statement: A list of the amounts paid and received during a period (usually a month) with a balance shown at the end of the amount that remains in the account.

Bankrupt: Someone who has been recognised by the courts as being unable to pay their debts.

Bonus: Additional money that is given to an employee on top of wages earned.

Cash flow: The amount of money coming in and going out of a business or your personal account.

Credit card: A card that can be used to buy goods. You can then pay a proportion of the amount each month or the whole balance on receipt of a statement. Monthly interest is charged on the unpaid amount.

Creditor: A person or company that money is owed to.

Debit card: A card that can be used for purchases instead of writing a cheque where the money is taken straight out of the bank account. Not a credit card.

Debt: An amount of money that is owed to a company or another person.

Debtor: Someone who owes money to a company or another person.

Direct debit: An instruction to the bank to pay a monthly or quarterly bill direct from a person's bank account.

Financial portfolio: A list of investments a person holds.

Store card: A credit card that can be used in a particular chain of stores. These cards have higher interest charges than bank credit cards.

Wage: The amount paid for work done.

RELATIONSHIPS

Co-dependency: A pattern of behaviour that makes you stay in an unhealthy relationship.

Compatibility: The beliefs, values and morals that you have in common.

Flings: Relationships that are not serious.

Infidelity: Being unfaithful within a serious relationship.

Introduction agencies: Also known as dating agencies.

Love profile/map: Your love profile of an ideal relationship and partner.

Monogamy: A committed relationship exclusive of all others.

Personal ads: Dating advertisements in the newspaper or online.

Rebound: Bouncing out of one relationship straight into another.

Resources

Body

UK

British Osteopathic Information
Tel: 01582 488455 (advice line)
Website: www.osteopathy.org.uk

British Nutrition Foundation
Tel: 0207 404 6504
Website: www.nutrition.org.uk

British Wheel of Yoga (send an sae)
1 Hamilton Place, Boston Road,
Sleaford, Lincolnshire NG34 7ES
Tel: 01529 303233
Website: www.bwy.org.uk

National Centre for Eating Disorders
54 New Road, Esher, Surrey,
KT10 9NO
Tel: 01372 469493
Website: www.eating-disorders.org.uk

Gyms
Cannons
Website:
www.cannons-health-club.co.uk

David Lloyd Clubs
Website: www.davidlloydclubs.co.uk

Holmes Place
Website: www.holmes-place.co.uk

LA Fitness
Website: www.lafitness.co.uk
To find your nearest trainer call
National Register of Personal Trainers
on 020 7407 9223 or go to
www.nrpt.co.uk

Walking
Website: www.walking.org

AUSTRALIA

Health & Fitness
Fitness tips
Website:
www.healthandfitness.com.au

Fitness Australia
Fitness tips
Website: www.fitnessaustralia.com.au

Personal trainers and gyms
Website: www.fitnessonline.com

CANADA

Canadian Council of Food and
Nutrition
Website: www.ccfn.ca

Healthy eating
Website: www.dieticians.ca

NEW ZEALAND

Everybody
Health and fitness tips
Website: www.everybody.co.nz

GymFit
Health, nutrition and fitness tips
Website: www.gymfit.co.nz

SOUTH AFRICA

Bodyline Fitness Academy
Website: www.bodyline.co.za

Fitness Zone
Gyms, fitness tips, stockists, and yoga
and Pilates.
Website: www.fitnesszone.co.za

USA

American Council on Exercise
Website: www.acefitness.org

Shape Magazine
Health and fitness tips
Website: www.shape.com

Yoga and Pilates information
Website: www.yogilates.com

Career

UK

Psychometric/personality test sites
Website: www.mindtools.com
Website: www.psychometric.co.uk
Website: www.brain.com

Online Careers Library
Website: www.careers.lon.ac.uk

Job help
Website: www.mad.co.uk

AUSTRALIA

Australian Job Search
Website: www.jobsearch.gov.au

Career Information Service
Website: www.myfuture.edu.au

CANADA

Canadian Employment Site
Website: www.canadiancareers.com

The Job Bus Canada
Website: www.jobbus.com

SOUTH AFRICA

Job Food
Website: www.jobfood.com

USA

Career One-stop for New Career
Paths
Website: www.careeronestop.org

Career Information Net
Website: www.acinet.org

Interviewing Tips
Website:
www.joblink-usa.com/interview

Finance

UK

Citizens Advice Bureau (CAB)
Offers free advice about credit and
money issues from 700 local bureaux.
Website: www.nacab.org.uk

Consumer Credit Counselling Service
(CCCS)
A free, confidential advice service for
people in debt.
Tel: 0800 138 1111
Website: www.cccs.co.uk

Credit Action
A national charity, which aims to help
people educate themselves about
money.
Tel: 01522 699777
Website: www.creditaction.org.uk

FCL Debt Clinic
A free, confidential helpline offering
advice and solutions, including
supervised arrangements with
creditors.
Tel: 0800 716239 (freephone helpline,
open 9.00 a.m. – 9.00 p.m.,
Monday–Friday)
Website: www.fcl.org.uk
Email: help@debtclinic.co.uk

National Debtline
Telephone service offering advice and
self-help information packs to those in
debt.
Tel: 0808 808 4000 (free and
confidential)
Website: www.nationaldebtline.co.uk

The UK Insolvency Helpline
An online resource with a freephone
helpline, which gives advice to people
in debt.
Tel: 0800 074 6918 (freephone helpline,
open 24 hours, all year round)
Website: www.insolvencyhelpline.co.uk
Email: info@insolvencyhelpline.co.uk

AUSTRALIA

Debt Management Foundation
Website:
www.debt-management-foundation.com

Legal Aid Commission
A non-profit organisation representing
Consumer Credit Counselling.
Tel: 1800 808 488
Website: www.legalaid.nsw.gov.au

CANADA

Website: www.canlaw.com
Tel: 1-888-527-8999

NEW ZEALAND

Citizens Advice Bureaux
Tel: 0800 367 222
Website: www.cab.org.nz

SOUTH AFRICA

South African Financial Services
Industry
Website: www.finforum.co.za

Ombudsman for Banking Services
Website: www.obssa.co.za

USA

Family Credit Counseling Corporation
Tel: 1 (800) 304 2369
Website: www.familycredithelp.org

Free advice on how to reduce debt.
Website:
www.800creditcarddebt.com

Relationships

UK

Relate
Couples counselling.
Website: www.relate.org.uk

BBC UK Relationships
Website:
www.bbc.co.uk/relationships

Dating
Website: www.match.com
Website: www.dateline.com

AUSTRALIA

Australian Relationship Support
Website: www.relationships.com.au

Cope
Website: www.cope.edu.au

CANADA

Canadian Counselling Association
Website: www.ccacc.ca

SOUTH AFRICA

Matrimony Online
Website: www.matrimony.co.za

USA

Council for Relationships
Relationship therapy.
Website:
www.councilforrelationships.org

Index

junk food 16, 22, 30, 36, 40, 50

King, Stephen 77

lattes 40
lethargy 39
letters of application 89–90
life plans 198
listening skills, active 181, 187, 188
loans 134
love profiles/maps 167–72, 197

meals
    size of 47
    skipping 29
mentors, career 86, 100
metabolic rate 29
mobile phones 127, 151
'Mr Right' 172
muscles 40

neediness 174
networking 85, 100
nuts 38

omega-3 fatty acids 38

paraphrasing 188
parents
    influence on your career 71–2
    influence on your eating habits 19–21
    influence on your money sense
        115–16
    influence on your relationship patterns
        168–70
past experiences, dealing with painful 173,
    196

personal trainers 45
personality tests 95, 99
physical exercise 16, 23–5
    aerobic 41–4
    finding time for 43–4
    and your heart rate 24–5, 31–2
    for the one-month body makeover 50–2
    recommended levels 24, 31, 43, 49
    strengthening work 40
    with your partner 47
planners 60–1
players 161
possessions, selling unwanted 150
posture 91
property 136, 145
    equity 136
protein 30, 36, 37
psychometric tests 95

quizzes
    about your career 58–61
    about your finances 106–9
    about your body 10–13
    about your relationship 158–61

raw foods 50
ready-made meals 40
recruitment agencies 100
rejectors 61
relationships 155–99
    admitting you have a problem 165
    arguments in 171, 181, 185–8, 192,
        199
    assessing your compatibility 176–8
    with attached lovers 174–5
    and bad partner choice 173–5
    beliefs/expectations about 167–72,
        196, 197